QUICK & EASY
QUILTS

QUICK & EASY
QUILTS

20 Machine Quilting Projects

Lynne Goldsworthy

Photography by
Jan Baldwin

The Taunton Press

To my long-suffering Welsh husband, Nigel, who has put up with me for 25 years (and my mad quilting obsession for five years!), and to my four children, Tom, Jack, Eve and Amy, who got stuck with their relatively normal Mum turning into that weird quilting lady.

First published in the United States in 2017 by

The Taunton Press
Inspiration for hands-on living®

The Taunton Press, Inc., 63 South Main Street,
PO Box 5506, Newtown, CT 06470-5506
email: tp@taunton.com

First published in Great Britain by Kyle Books,
an imprint of Kyle Cathie Ltd.

10 9 8 7 6 5 4 3 2 1

Text © 2016 Lynne Goldsworthy
Design © 2016 Kyle Books
Photographs © 2016 Jan Baldwin
Illustrations © 2016 Bess Harding

Project Editor: **Tara O'Sullivan**
U.S. Editor: **Karen Bolesta**
Copy Editor: **Lin Clements**
Editorial Assistant: **Amberley Lowis**
Designer: **Lucy Gowans**
Photographer: **Jan Baldwin**
Illustrator: **Bess Harding**
Prop Stylist: **Claudia Bryant**
Production: **Lisa Pinnell**

Library of Congress Cataloging-in-Publication Data
Names: Goldsworthy, Lynne, author.
Title: Quick & easy quilts : 20 machine-quilting projects / Lynne
  Goldsworthy.
Other titles: Quick and easy quilts
Description: Newtown, CT : The Taunton Press, Inc., 2018.
Identifiers: LCCN 2017026662 | ISBN 9781631869143
Subjects: LCSH: Patchwork--Patterns. | Quilting--Patterns. | Machine
  quilting--Patterns.
Classification: LCC TT835 .G659 2018 | DDC 746.46--dc23
LC record available at https://lccn.loc.gov/2017026662

Color reproduction by ALTA London

Printed and bound in China by C & C Offset Printing Co., Ltd

CONTENTS

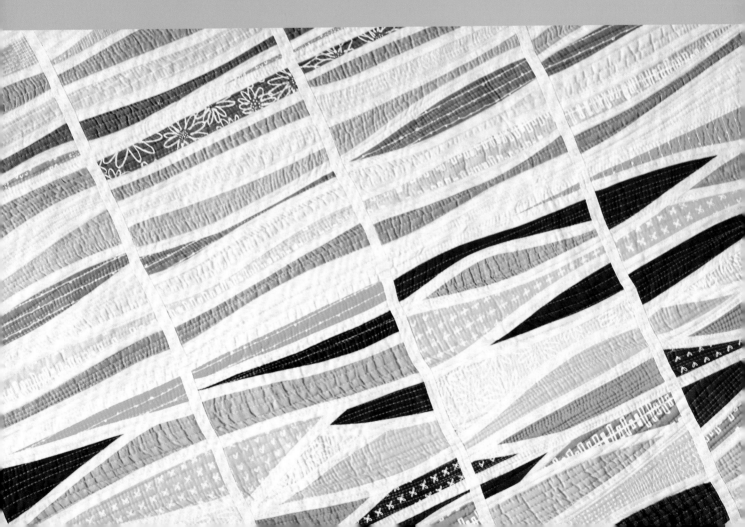

INTRODUCTION

When I first learned patchwork as a child,

it was using paper hexagons, wrapping fabric around them and hand-sewing them together. That simple method of piecing quilt tops has not changed since the days of the American pioneers, whose creations probably spring to mind when we think of traditional quilts. The hours and hours of work that went into them can be seen in every stitch.

With the advent of sewing machines, it became possible to create quilts much faster. Templates and scissors were replaced with rotary cutters, cutting mats and strip piecing, all of which helped speed up the whole process. These days, long-arm machines and dedicated home sewing machines mean large quilts can be pieced and quilted at home, in a fraction of the time it would take by hand. Of course, many people still love to piece and quilt by hand, but this book is designed for anyone who would like to make a quilt in a few days rather than a few weeks or months.

There are so many beautiful new quilting fabric lines coming out all the time and so much inspiration on Instagram, Facebook, Pinterest and all the other social media platforms out there, that I'm always impatient to delve into the next quilt, the next fabric line, the next design. So, although I certainly appreciate the peacefulness of hand-sewing and admire beautiful hand-piecing and -quilting done by others, I'm all about the speed. And so is this book.

It is important to say that speed doesn't mean sloppy techniques or finishes. You still need an accurate ¼in seam, you're still aiming for your points to match and it's always good to see a really well mitered binding corner. You'll find that the projects in this book are designed to be made with a bit more speed and possibly a few more shortcuts than most quilts.

ABBREVIATIONS

F8TH = FAT EIGHTH
A cut of fabric approximately 9in x 21in–22in if cut in a shop using imperial measurements, or 25cm x 56cm if cut in a shop using metric measurements, where the cut will be slightly bigger.

F16TH = FAT SIXTEENTH
A cut of fabric approximately 9in x 11in if cut in a shop using imperial measurements, or 25cm x 30cm if cut in a shop using metric measurements, where the cut will be slightly bigger.

FPP = FOUNDATION PAPER PIECING
This technique is described in more detail in the Techniques section (page 16). It is a form of piecing using a paper template as a foundation for the block.

FQ = FAT QUARTER
A cut of fabric approximately 18in x 21in–22in if cut in a shop using imperial measurements, or 50cm x 56cm if cut in a shop using metric measurements, where the cut will be slightly bigger.

HST = HALF-SQUARE TRIANGLE
For the projects in this book, this is a square block unit made up of two right-angle triangles.

LOF = LENGTH OF FABRIC
A strip of fabric cut along the length of the fabric, i.e. cut parallel to the selvage.

QAYG = QUILT AS YOU GO
A method of making quilts where the blocks are quilted first then joined together.

RST = RIGHT SIDES TOGETHER
Fabrics are generally placed right sides together when piecing.

WOF = WIDTH OF FABRIC
A strip of fabric cut across the width of the fabric, i.e. from one selvage to the other.

WST = WRONG SIDES TOGETHER
Although fabrics are usually pieced right sides together, there are times, such as when making binding, when the fabric will be pressed wrong sides together.

EQUIPMENT AND MATERIALS

Although all quilting equipment is available online, I always suggest buying your equipment from a reputable local quilt shop if you have one. The shop owner will have a wealth of knowledge and experience and will be able to advise you on the equipment that will best suit you. As an added bonus, you can't beat strolling through the bolts of fabric, seeing the colors and prints in real life, mixing and matching fabrics you can hold and see and chatting to the owner about your latest project. Below is a list of the equipment and materials you might need for quilting. I also make sure I have a trash bin and a scrap bin right next to where I work. Odd threads, corners of fabric and selvages can go straight into the trash bin, and scraps can go into a scrap bin to be sorted and stored later.

Fabric

I almost always use 100% cotton for my projects. Different manufacturers' cottons will vary slightly in weight and drape, and you may find some fabrics that are made from organic cotton. Buy quilting fabric in your local quilt shop, online or at shows. Buy pre-cuts, fat quarters or yardage. New fabric lines are being designed and released constantly—some modern, some traditional—and the choice is seemingly endless. Fabric is the fun part of quilting for me—it inspires all of my projects and brings color and pattern into my life.

Thread

There are so many wonderful threads to choose from in all the colors of the rainbow. You may find that certain brands suit your machine better than others. I would suggest buying quality thread because cheap thread breaks and frays constantly. My brand of choice is Aurifil®, whose threads come

in various weights. I use two weights 99 percent of the time.
• 50wt (orange spool) for piecing. I tend to buy mostly neutrals for piecing—cream, beige, light grey and dark grey cover most piecing needs.
• 40wt (green spool) for quilting. Since this will show on the outside of your work, you can have fun choosing from the many, many colors of thread, including beautiful variegated threads that change color along the length.

Batting

There are lots of different types of quilt batting. The best way to choose the batting suitable for your project is to go to your local quilt shop and inquire about the pros and cons of the different types they stock. Some are loftier and cozier, some are flatter and better suited to wall hangings and quilts that will lie on top of other bedding. After you have made a few

quilts you will probably have one or two preferred battings that you use for most quilts. I use Warm and Natural® for a wall hanging or bed quilt and Heirloom 80:20® for a quilt that will be used for cuddling.

Scissors

You really need a minimum of three pairs of scissors, but you may find you end up with more over time. You need one decent pair of fabric shears, a pair of embroidery scissors with pointed blades for snipping small threads and a pair of scissors for use on paper. Good fabric scissors may become blunt if you use them on paper.

Fabric Markers

There are many dedicated fabric marking pens and pencils on the market, but the ones I use most of all were never in fact designed for use on fabric. They are called Frixion® Erasable Marker Pens and can be bought in office supply stores and supermarkets. They are designed so that the heat generated by the friction of the eraser on the end erases the mark. The mark can also be erased by applying heat using an iron. You should always test this on the back of any fabrics you are using because the pen may leave a "ghost" mark. Apparently, the marks may come back if the quilt gets cold (like if it were shipped in the hold of plane). The marks can be erased again using an iron.

Hera Marker

This is a plastic tool I use to mark straight lines on my quilt tops for quilting. It works a little like running the curved, blunt end of a knife along the top of your quilt to mark a line. When using a hera marker and when quilting lines marked with a hera marker, having the light (for example, from a window) to one side of you rather than in front of or behind you helps the lines to stand out.

Quilting Rulers

There are many sizes and shapes of rulers on the market, but a beginner should start with a standard quilt ruler, which measures 6½in x 24½in. This should be marked in inches and should be a dedicated quilting ruler, made of strong, transparent plastic. I like the rulers with non-slip backs because these help to prevent the ruler from sliding around as you make a long cut. In time, you may wish to invest in more rulers. I have a 4½in x 12½in ruler that is more manageable when making smaller cuts. There are also square rulers that help when squaring up blocks and many specialty rulers, such as Dresden wedge rulers, kaleidoscope rulers and curved rulers.

Cutting Mat

You may end up with multiple cutting mats over time, but a beginner should start with one large mat. I'd suggest 18in x 24in if you have a surface to fit that size mat. It should be marked in inches on at least one side, and it is useful if the mat also has other markings such as 45- and 60-degree angle lines. In time, you may want to buy other mats, such as a smaller mat for taking to classes, a larger mat if you have a big enough surface to use it or a rotating mat, which is fantastic for trimming blocks and small shapes. Although cutting mats are self-healing, after repeated use, your mat will need to be replaced, especially if it starts to split in the places where you cut most or develops deep grooves.

Die Cutters

Accuquilt® and Sizzix® make the most popular die cutters, although there are many more on the market and some that are even computer programmed so that any shape can be cut. The mechanical cutters come with individual cutting dies, one for each shape you wish to cut. These machines cut quickly and accurately and can cut six to eight layers at one time. I find that they can be a huge time-saver and have often used them on large projects where the same few shapes are being repeated, such as 2½in squares and half-square triangles. In this book, I used an Accuquilt circles die for The Planets Mini Quilt (page 100). The circles die I used has 5in, 3in and 2in circles and this saved a lot of time during the cutting process.

Rotary Cutter

Rotary cutters come in three sizes, with blades in metric sizes of 28mm, 45mm and 60mm. I use the standard 45mm size, although you may prefer a 28mm for more detailed work. Rainbow

Leaves Runner (page 96) uses a zigzag blade for the rotary-cut shapes. When buying a cutter, it is always worth buying a few spare blades. You can find packs of decent blades at a good price online and at quilt shows, but don't buy blades from a hardware store because they are not suitable for fabric.

Pins

Selecting pins is a matter of personal preference. There are many different shapes, sizes and varieties on the market. I like pins that are quite long and slim—they often come in circular packs and can have pretty shapes on the top, such as flowers and hearts.

Basting Pins

These pins are used for basting (tacking) a quilt sandwich together (the three layers of a quilt: back, batting and quilt top). They are just like safety pins but have a curved side, which makes it easier to pin through the layers.

Binding Clips

These little clips appeared on the market relatively recently and are a great alternative to pins in a lot of situations. I use Clover Wonder Clips®, but other brands are available. I use them for attaching binding, and I also used them in the Scrappy Trees Quilt (page 68) for holding multiple layers together.

Basting Spray

Basting spray is a great way to speed up the quilt sandwich process. I prefer to use spray rather than pins on any project up to about 40in square. (Beyond that I find that pins are easier to use and hold the project together better.) The spray I use is called 505® Spray and Fix and is made by Odif.

Needles (hand)

Your choice of needle for hand-sewing is another of those matters of personal preference. Most quilters prefer a regular length needle. I like long sashiko or straw needles because smaller ones make my hands cramp.

Seam Ripper

Seam rippers tend to come free with sewing machines and sewing kits, but I'd advise investing in a quality seam ripper and replacing it when the blade becomes blunt. With a bit of practice, you can slide the sharp point of the seam ripper in between the two layers of fabric and run it along the seam, taking out all the stitches as you go; just be careful not to rip your fabric.

Tweezers

Although not usually a quilting tool, I keep tweezers handy at all times for grabbing those tiny threads that get stuck when you rip out a seam and can't be bothered to de-thread.

Sewing Machine

When you first start quilting, before you have decided if the bug has really bitten you, you might want to look online for a second-hand machine. Once you know you're committed to quilting for the longer term, do your research before buying a machine to find the one that really suits your needs. The majority of the time you will use just the straight stitch so you don't need (and will probably never use) hundreds of fancy stitches, but most modern computerized machines come with them anyway. Features that you might want to consider include:
• A larger throat space for quilting.
• Quality built-in lighting.

• A button that chooses whether the needle stops in an up or down position.
• An automatic thread cutter.
• A needle threader.

Sewing Machine Feet

Sewing machines tend to come with a whole host of feet, which you may never use or even understand. There are a few indispensable feet for a quilter, on top of the basic foot that comes with the machine:
• A quarter-inch foot for accurate ¼in seams. I like the ones with a metal guide on the right-hand side to guide the edge of your fabric as you piece.
• A walking foot for straight line quilting and binding—these are built in to some machines.
• A free-motion quilting foot for freehand quilting.

Needles (machine)

This is another item worth spending a bit more money on—cheap needles, like cheap thread, will break, skip stitches, blunt quickly and snag fabric. I use Superior® Titanium-Coated Topstitch needles, which I think are the best on the market. They can cost up to three times as much as a regular sewing needle but last at least five times as long due to their specially coated tip, which stays sharper much longer. Needles should be replaced if they start skipping stitches, pushing the fabric down into the needle plate or if they sound as though they are becoming blunt.

Needle Plate

Many machines have two needle plates as standard. One has a wider opening, tends to be the standard fitted plate and is used for any stitch where the needle moves side to side, such as

a zigzag stitch. The other needle plate is called a straight stitch needle plate and has a small circular opening for the needle to go through. This can only be used for straight stitches, where the needle does not move from side to side. Some machines automatically change the width of the needle hole depending on the stitch you choose on the machine. You may wish to consider fitting or buying a straight stitch plate if you find that your fabrics are constantly getting pushed down into the needle hole on the regular plate. This can also be caused by using a needle that is too thick for the fabric being sewn, especially when you have a lightweight fabric.

Feed Dogs

These are the teeth underneath the needle plate that feed the fabric through the machine. Feed dogs are usually lowered for free-motion quilting. You can find the instructions in your machine's manual.

Tension Dial

Sometimes the tension on your machine will start to become unbalanced, forming loops on the top or bottom of the work. If this happens, try the following steps:
• Re-thread your machine.
• Confirm that you have the same thread in the top and bobbin.
• Check whether you need a new needle.
If you haven't solved the problem, you can adjust the tension yourself—consult your sewing machine manual and try to correct the problem. If you find this is a persistent problem that you cannot fix yourself, have the machine serviced and explain the tension issue to the technician.

Bobbin Winder

I bought a little battery-operated portable bobbin winder at a quilt show recently. This has been one of those useful little gadgets that helps to speed up the whole quiltmaking process because you don't have to stop what you're doing, unthread the machine and watch a bobbin wind. You can just let the little machine wind bobbins while you continue with your project.

Quilting Extension Table

A quilting extension table is an optional extra on some machines and is very useful for holding a quilt steady and raising it up to the sewing surface as you quilt it.

Long-Arm Quilting Machine

Long-arm machines cost many thousands of dollars and usually need their own dedicated room, so most quilters won't have their own. They consist of a large frame to hold the quilt and a sewing machine that can be "driven" around the quilt to quilt the lines, rather than moving the quilt around under the needle as you would with a home sewing machine. You can find long-arm quilters locally or online who will machine-quilt your projects for you.

Iron and Ironing Board

Each quilter will need to find the iron that suits them the best. I prefer a heavy iron that has a steam function, but other quilters prefer a lighter iron and still others will never use steam on their projects. You tend to get better results with a good iron rather than a very cheap one. I have never really liked pressing my quilting on an ironing board. I find I get much better results if I put an old towel on a flat surface like a tabletop and press on that. I also have a little filing cabinet on wheels with an old towel on top just under my sewing table. I wheel it out when I'm working on something like foundation paper piecing, where I need to press seams between each step.

Spray Starch

This is available in supermarkets and is useful for helping curved and stubborn seams and blocks to lie flat. As with steam in the iron, be careful not to stretch your work out of shape if you use starch when pressing.

Lint Roller

These are available in most supermarkets, and I use them constantly. I prefer the ones with the peel-off sticky sheets. I use them for pulling threads from a ripped-out seam, for removing stray threads from a finished block or quilt and for removing cat hairs or dust from a project.

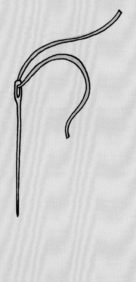

TECHNIQUES

Imperial or Metric?

Most quilters use the imperial measuring system (think inches, not centimeters). The projects in this book are made and measured using inches, half inches, quarter inches and eighths of an inch. I have provided metric conversions for the overall size of the project and for the amount of yardage needed in the project "You Will Need" lists, in case you buy fabrics from an international source. These conversions usually include a margin of error or rounding and have only been included to give an idea of the sizes of finished projects and the amount of fabric needed. They should not be used to convert measurements in the patterns for making up blocks and projects. The projects have been designed and written in imperial and will not piece together accurately if converted into approximately similar metric measurements.

Accurate Piecing

For me, the four most important skills in quilting are accurate cutting, an accurate and consistent seam allowance, good pressing and "nested" seams. If you can take the time to master these four techniques, you will find that your piecing will speed up because points will match first time, seams won't need to be ripped out and projects will go together smoothly the first time (or most of the time).

Washing Fabrics

Before starting any new project, take a moment to consider whether to pre-wash your fabrics. As a general rule, I don't pre-wash, as most good quilting fabrics will be colorfast, but I would consider pre-washing if I was using a mix of light colors with very strong dark colors. You can pre-wash the dark colors with a color catcher and possibly even a tester piece of white fabric in the machine, as this will let you know whether the darker fabrics are colorfast or might need a bit more washing before you start to piece.

Accurate Cutting

Once you have pressed your fabrics, it is time to cut. Your essential tools are a good cutting mat, a good quilting ruler and a rotary cutter with a sharp blade. I talked more about choosing these items in the equipment section. The old quilters' adage is measure twice, cut once. It is always worth taking the extra second or two needed to make sure you're cutting the right piece at the right size. Nothing is more disheartening than cutting that last essential piece of fabric slightly too small and wondering whether your local quilt shop carries that fabric and is open at 7pm on a Friday night. Fabrics are usually ready for cutting in four different formats:

- Yardage (a decent sized piece cut from the bolt).
- Fat quarters or fat eighths.
- Pre-cuts, such as packs of 10in squares.
- Scraps.

✦ CUTTING YARDAGE

When cutting yardage, you will generally need to have it folded twice to fit on your cutting mat. Don't assume that any of the folds in the fabric are good, straight folds—you may need to open out the fabric, press away the strong fold created by the bolt, re-fold and fold in half again so that the selvages and the folds all sit parallel to one another. The following instructions assume right-handed cutting, so reverse these for left-handed cutting.

1 Align the folds and selvages with the horizontal lines on your mat and align your ruler with the vertical lines on your mat. This will ensure that any cuts made across the full width of this fabric have the best chance of coming out straight.

2 Trim the left-hand edge as follows. Space your left hand out across your ruler so that it holds the top, middle and bottom steady. Place the index finger of your right hand on the top of the rotary cutter and make a smooth, confident cut away from you (Fig 1 on page 14). Don't rush this, don't saw

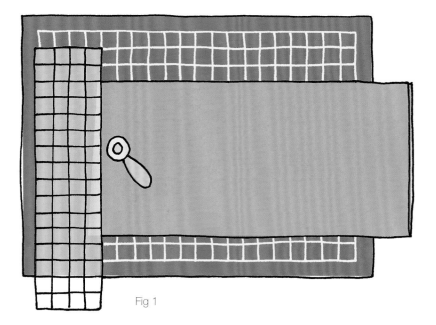

Fig 1

up and down and, most of all, don't cut towards yourself, ever. Don't look away from the rotary cutter while you're cutting and don't talk to your daughter about why she hasn't done her homework or you might accidentally take a small piece of finger off and have to go to the doctor to have it sorted out. Ask me how I know...

3 Once you've made that first cut, you can continue moving your ruler to the right, double-checking each time that you're cutting the right width and then cutting width of fabric strips from the yardage, which may then be sub-cut into smaller pieces. Quilting wisdom suggests you should use only the ruler as a measuring tool and not the mat, but I like to use both as a sort of double insurance policy. If you count 2½in both on your ruler and on your mat, you are more likely to make the right cut.

4 When you become more confident, you can fold the yardage in half again lengthwise so that both yardage ends are being cut at the same time—eight layers in all. Eight is probably a good maximum to aim for, but cut fewer if you find your accuracy decreases with more layers. If your rotary cutter is skipping or missing places, you may not be pressing down hard enough. But, if you are applying a reasonable amount of pressure (not excessive), and the blade is still not cutting consistently through all the layers, then it is time for a replacement blade. You probably need to replace your blade after each decent-sized quilt project; you will find that a new blade makes your cutting quicker and more accurate.

✦ CUTTING FQS AND F8THS

A fat quarter (FQ) is usually 18in x 22in and a fat eighth (F8th) 9in x 22in. When cutting FQs or F8ths, don't assume that the pre-cut has been cut straight or is the perfect size. As mentioned before, you can cut across four folded layers, once you've checked that the folds are parallel. Alternatively, you can open up the pre-cut, press it flat and cut it in the same way as you did for yardage, aligning the fabric with the horizontal lines, making that first vertical cut to trim the left-hand edge and then making more parallel vertical cuts as needed. Once those strips need to be cut into smaller pieces, rotate the fabric so that it once again aligns with the horizontal lines on the mat and make vertical cuts from there.

✦ CUTTING PRE-CUTS

Many pre-cuts, such as 2½in strips, 10in squares and 5in squares, come with pinked (zigzag) edges. Before you start cutting them up, make sure you check the following points:
• Is the square or strip a full, accurate 10in, 5in or 2½in size?
• Do the pinked edges need to be removed?
• Are you going to use the outside or the inside of the pinked ridges as your cutting and piecing guide? Where there is sufficient fabric, I prefer to remove these pinked edges as I find they can be confusing and inconsistent to work with.
• For pre-cuts without pinked edges, the same rule applies —don't assume that they are the stated size and always double-check so that your piecing will be as accurate as possible.

✦ CUTTING SCRAPS

Scraps and leftovers are some of the most fun fabrics to piece with because you can squeeze so much variety into one project, and many of them hold memories of earlier quilts or projects. Because you are working with lots of little random bits of fabric of all different shapes and sizes often crammed into a plastic bin all together, scraps can take a little longer to cut. But the same basic rules apply—press them first, align with the mat to make the first vertical cut to trim the left-hand edge, then align that cut with the horizontal lines on the mat to make subsequent cuts.

✦ DIE CUTTERS

I talked about die cutters on page 9, and they're worth mentioning here, too, because they are fast, easy and accurate to use. These cutters can also be helpful for anyone with shoulder, elbow, wrist or hand issues, which make it difficult to do a lot of rotary cutting.

Accurate Seam Allowance

If you buy a new sewing machine or a new sewing machine foot, or if you find that your piecing is becoming less accurate, it is time to do the seam allowance test. Step one is to throw out the notion that you need to measure the width of the seam allowance. That won't give you accurate piecing, but this method will. Mastering this is the most important thing you can do to improve the speed and accuracy of your piecing.

1 Cut two 4½in squares. Sew them together using some kind of guide for your seam allowance. This guide can be a ¼in foot, several pieces of masking tape stuck to the top of your machine (which you can guide your fabrics along as you piece) or a line marked on your machine with a permanent marker.

2 Press the piece open and measure the width. It should measure 8½in. If it is slightly wider than 8½in, your seam allowance is slightly too small. If it is slightly narrower, your seam allowance is slightly too big.

3 Adjust your seam by a minute amount. This could mean moving the needle position on your machine, if your needle position is adjustable on your machine. It could mean moving the masking tape or the permanent pen line (these lines are usually removable with some kind of solvent such as nail polish remover). It could mean adjusting very slightly the

distance between the edge of your fabric and the edge of your ¼in foot, by the width of a thread or two.

4 Cut and sew another two 4½in squares together and keep adjusting and testing until your sewn piece measures 8½in wide each time.

Pressing

There are two steps to pressing a seam. The first is to "set" the seam. Here, you press on top of the seam line before the piece is opened up. This sets the thread into the fabric and will create a straighter pressed line. The second is to press the sewn seam open and flat. Seams can be pressed towards the darker fabric, away from the bulkier side or open, as preferred. I tend to press open for a really clean crisp seam line, to one side when seams will need to meet and nest and to one side for speed. I have no hard and fast rule and my choice can depend on how rushed I feel and how anxious I am to get a section finished.

When pressing a seam open, remember that quilters press, not iron. That means that you shouldn't move the iron around over the top of your block, distorting the shape. Instead, lift the iron up and down to press the seams flat. If you use steam for a flatter seam, be even more careful to avoid distorting the shape of the block or fabric you are pressing. Spray starch can also help get a seam really flat or persuade curved or stubborn seams to do what they're told—but, again, be careful not to stretch blocks out of shape.

Nesting Seams

Once you've mastered accurate cutting, seam allowances and pressing, the final key technique to master is that of nesting seams. A four-patch quilt like the Kodachrome Quilt (see page 58) is good practice for a beginner quilter because every single seam should meet. I'm not giving you any kind of guarantee that every single seam *did* meet on my version but I hope most of them did. The theory is simple: when two seams meet, the seam allowance on one should go in one direction and the seam allowance on the other should go in the other direction, with the seam lines as close as possible so they nest (or abut) together.

If you are making a quilt with multiple rows of four-patch units, you can either press the seams in one direction in the first and third rows and the other direction in the second and fourth rows or, as I did with Kodachrome's checkerboard

Fig 2

layout, press all seams towards the darker fabric in each block. When the rows of the block are then sewn together, you can feel the joining point by pressing the two pieces together at the point where the seams meet and they will nest together (Fig 2).

Before you start to tear your hair out because you are not achieving 100 percent perfection at the meeting of every seam, remember these three very important quilting tips:
• Perfection is overrated. You will be the only person who will ever notice any little imperfections in your quilts.
• Quilters like to leave "humility blocks" in their quilts as a reminder that we are only human and not perfect, so any mistake or missed point can be your contribution to that great and noble tradition.
• You do not need to rip out every cut-off point if it's not noticeable from 5ft away.

Chain Piecing

Chain piecing is a method of piecing lots of small pieces one after the other. It is a much faster piecing technique, with each piece being fed into the machine right after the previous one has been sewn without cutting the thread between each piece. This creates a long chain of pieces that can be snipped apart by cutting the threads between each one (Fig 3).

Foundation Paper Piecing

Foundation paper piecing is used for several projects in this book. Once you master it, it has the great advantage of being a quick, easy and accurate way to make blocks

in a relatively short space of time. The piecing lines are printed onto the front of the foundation paper and the block is pieced onto the back so the final piece will be the front in reverse. I like to pre-cut my fabrics for foundation piecing where possible. They do not need to be cut accurately as in regular piecing, and I tend to aim for each piece to be at least ½in more than is needed all around, so that I never add a piece that ends up just a little bit too small. A number of patterns in this book use foundation paper piecing for half-square triangle (HST) units, which makes multiple numbers of HSTs quickly and easily without the slow process of trimming at the end. Here are the steps for basic foundation paper piecing.

1 Start with a printed template. Templates can be scanned and printed or traced onto tracing, typing, newsprint or copy paper; you also can trace templates on card stock. The numbers represent the order in which the sections will be pieced. The dashed line around the outside is the trimming line once the block is pieced (Fig 4).

2 Flip the template over and align the fabric you are using for section 1 so that it covers all of section 1 plus at least ¼in on each side. The wrong side of the fabric should be facing the back of the template (Fig 5).

3 Align and pin the piece you are using for section 2 with right sides together and the edge aligned with the first piece. This way, when the seam is sewn and the fabric is flipped over, it will cover all of section 2 plus at least ¼in all around (Fig 6).

4 Shorten the stitch length to 14 to 18 stitches per inch for lightweight templates and up to 22 stitches per inch for heavyweight templates. Sew along the seam line between sections 1 and 2 and just beyond that line at each end (Fig 7).

5 Trim your seam allowance to ¼in. Flip that fabric over and press flat (Fig 8).

6 Repeat the process with the pieces for sections 3, 4 and 5 (Fig 9).

7 Trim the paper and fabric to the dashed line (Fig 10).

8 To finish the block, remove the papers by folding over at each seam line and tearing away, starting with the highest number and finishing with the lowest.

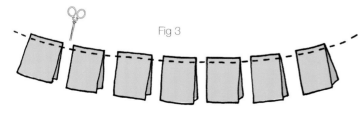

Fig 3

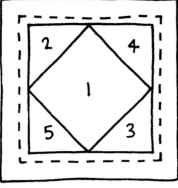

Fig 4

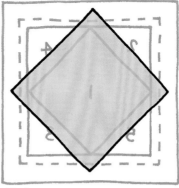

Fig 5

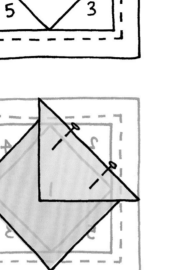

Fig 6

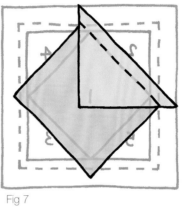

Fig 7

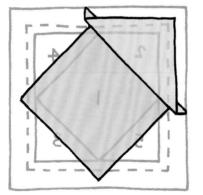

Fig 8

Fig 9

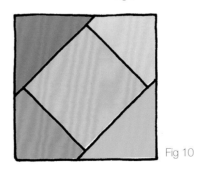

Fig 10

Making a Quilt Back

There is no special magic to making a quilt back for the quilts in this book. In most cases, you simply cut the backing piece into two equal lengths, remove the selvages and sew into one double-width piece along the long sides using a ½in seam. Press that seam open or to one side, as preferred. The back should be about 8in longer and wider than the quilt top, so the width can be trimmed at this stage to make the back more manageable at the basting stage.

Some fabric shops will carry special extra-wide fabrics for making quilt backs—usually 108in wide, and these make the whole process of backing a quilt much quicker and easier, although the choice of prints is, of course, much more limited than the choice for 44in wide fabrics. If using a wider backing fabric, you will need to adjust your fabric requirements accordingly, rather than using the amount listed in the project "You Will Need" lists.

When using a large-scale print for the back, I like to align the pattern across the fabric join as you might do when hanging wallpaper. To do this, you need to find out the size of the repeat. If it is 8in, add 8in to the fabric requirements for the back of the quilt. As before, cut the fabric into two equal lengths and remove selvages. Fold back about 1in along the long side of one of the pieces and press flat. Take this over to the other backing piece and align the print from one piece to the next. Pin along the folded edge. Finally, topstitch along that folded edge in a thread that matches the quilt back as closely as possible.

Making a Quilt Sandwich

Assembling the three layers of a quilt together, often called making a quilt sandwich, can be done in various ways. The most common are basting (tacking) the layers together, using a spray adhesive or pinning. The process can be rather tedious and backbreaking. If you don't have a big table to do this on, you could find a local quilt shop that does. They will often let you use their tables for preparing quilts, either free or for a small charge.

1 First press and lay out the quilt back, right side down. Pull it flat but don't over stretch it. Tape it to your work surface using cellophane or masking tape (depending on whether the surface is plastic, glass or wood). Lay the batting on top. This should be roughly the same size as the backing, or maybe a fraction smaller so that you can see the edge of the backing all round. Smooth out the batting until it is as flat as you can make it. Finally, add the quilt top, right side up, and smooth it until it is as flat as you can get it without pulling it out of shape.

2 You can now either pin or spray-baste the layers together. For a smaller project (up to about 40in square), I would use spray. Fold back half of the quilt top and batting, spray all over the batting and lay it back down flat. Smooth it as flat as you can. Repeat for the other half of the quilt. Now repeat that part of the process using the quilt top but again spraying onto the batting and not the fabric. If pinning, use basting pins and pin all over, starting in the center and working your way out to the edges—aim for somewhere between 3in and 5in apart. The closer they are together, the less likely the layers are going to shift when you quilt.

Marking a Quilt

If you are doing an all-over stipple or other free-motion design, you may not wish to mark your quilt top for quilting. I like to mark mine when I am quilting straight lines as I find it keeps them straighter than just following seam lines. I mark with a hera marker, which I use to draw the lines along the side of my ruler as if I were using a pen.

Quilting

When your quilt top has been pieced, you have three options for quilting your quilt:
• The easiest but most expensive is to send it out to be quilted by a long-arm quilter. You will need to have an in-depth discussion about the design you would like to see, the cost of having it quilted and the thread to be used. This is a fantastic solution for people who don't have time to quilt their quilts or who don't enjoy the quilting part of the process.

• You can free-motion quilt your quilt. Lower the feed dogs, attach the free-motion quilting foot, place your quilt under the needle, draw up the bottom thread to the top so that the threads can be buried at a later stage and move the quilt around under the needle to create beautiful quilting designs. This method takes practice but is great fun to do. You can practice by drawing your designs out on paper first and stitching over them with an unthreaded machine.

• My favorite method of quilting is straight line quilting, which gives the quilt a uniform texture throughout and is quick and easy to do. I tend to use a slightly longer stitch length for machine quilting. The longer the stitch, the faster the process. You need to attach a walking foot so that all three layers will be pulled through at the same time. If you start a little bit off the edge of the quilt top and finish a little bit off the edge at the end, any threads that tangle on the back will be removed when the quilt is trimmed.

One thing to keep in mind when deciding how to quilt your quilt is how it is going to be used. If it is for a child to snuggle, the quilt will be softer and more cuddly if there is less quilting. Dense quilting will give a stiffer texture to a quilt so that makes it a good choice for wall hangings. For a quilt that will lie on top of a bed, something in between a little quilting and a lot of quilting is a good choice. You also need to check the minimum distance between quilting lines for the batting you are using because this varies from batting to batting.

Squaring Up

Once your quilt is quilted, you will need to trim it to size. You are aiming to trim it to the size of the quilt top, removing excess batting and backing, and making sure the sides are square. Lay your longest ruler along the quilt edge so that you cut long straight lines. I place my mat on the diagonal so that I have the longest cutting surface possible. Sometimes the true edge of the blocks falls inside and outside of the ruler as you trim, but I think the quilt will look better if the edges are straight so you can cut right across these sections. Once you reach the corner, make sure you align the horizontal lines on your ruler with the previously trimmed edge so that your corner is square.

Making Binding Strips

Binding can be single-fold or double-fold and can be bias or straight. It can also be made from different widths of fabric. I find the quickest and easiest binding to make is double-fold, straight cut, straight join binding. Preparing the strips is easy, as follows.

Cut as many 2½in x width of fabric strips as are suggested by the project instructions. Remove the selvages and sew the strips together end to end. Many quilters like to use a diagonal (45-degree) seam, but I find a straight seam quicker and easier. Press in half wrong sides together all along the length. The double-fold strip is now ready to use.

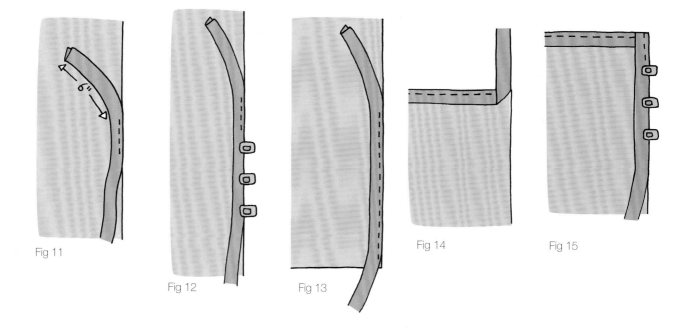

Fig 11

Fig 12

Fig 13

Fig 14

Fig 15

Binding

Binding is the final stage in the quiltmaking process, the part where you're nearly there. For that reason, I think it is the most fun part because you're about to see your finished quilt. I use clips to hold the binding in place and machine-sew my binding to the front of the quilt, fold it over to the back and then machine-sew the back down (see Figs 11–19 for the sequence). Many people prefer to hand-sew the back down—that is a matter of personal preference. Use a walking foot when attaching binding.

1 Start by clipping or pinning a piece of double-fold binding to the front of the quilt with the binding edge aligned with the edge of the quilt. You need a "tail" of about 6in before you start sewing. Start about halfway down one side. Sew about an inch or two using a ¼in seam and a stitch length of about 8 stitches per inch, then stop and remove the quilt from the machine (Fig 11).

2 Lay the quilt out on a tabletop. Do not pull or stretch it; let it lie flat but nice and relaxed. Clip the binding to the edge all the way to the next corner with one clip every 6in or so (Fig 12). Clipping it in this way prevents the edges of the quilt from becoming wavy as they are pulled through the machine. Sew from your starting point down the rest of that side until you come towards the corner. Stop exactly ¼in from the quilt edge and backstitch a few stitches to secure (Fig 13).

3 Rotate the quilt so that the next edge will be in the right direction to be sewn, flip the binding up as shown in Fig 14 and finger-press the diagonal fold.

4 Now fold the binding down so that it aligns with the exact top and side edges of the quilt, and sew a few stitches. Repeat the process of laying it out and clipping the binding to the next edge (Fig 15).

5 Continue this process around all four sides of the quilt until you are about 12in away from where you started. At this point, stop and lay the two tails of binding along the quilt edge until they meet. Where they meet, fold them each back, finger-press the seam line on each piece and trim to a seam allowance of approximately ½in. Pull the two tails up and over to the machine, bringing the ends together, right sides together. Shorten your stitch length and sew the seam. Finger-press open and lay the binding back down along the edge of the quilt (Fig 16). Sew the final stitches so that the whole binding is attached (Fig 17).

6 You can now machine-sew the binding to the back. Flip the quilt over and turn over the first section of binding. By feeling the front of the quilt, you need to ensure that you sew along the edge of the binding folded to the back, while not sewing on the binding fabric on the front. Once again, start in the middle of one of the sides and sew towards the corner, pulling over lengths of binding as you go and always feeling the front of the quilt to make sure your stitching is not sewing through the binding on the front. You can clip the folded

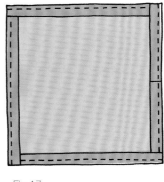

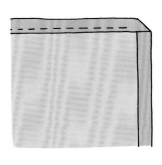

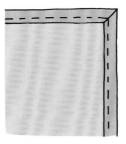

Fig 16

Fig 17

Fig 18

Fig 19

binding down with clips if you find that easier or you can fold as you go. Once you are close to the corner, pull the next side of binding out so that the corner of the binding comes to a neat 45-degree point (Fig 18).

7 Fold this piece back over the quilt to make a mitered corner. Again, clip this corner if you find it easier but I find it sufficient just to hold it as I sew towards it. Once you get to the stitch before you hit this mitered area, hand-crank the machine so that you are sure the needle will slot right down into this corner. Once the needle has caught the corner, you can turn the quilt with the needle embedded into the corner, then continue sewing the next side (Fig 19). Continue this process on all four sides and all four corners until you have finished.

8 The process is the same if you are hand-sewing the back of the binding, but sew using a slipstitch or blind stitch along the entire edge of the binding, carefully mitering the corners as you go.

Tidying Up

The final step in making a quilt is to tidy up the whole quilt. Fold the quilt in half and half again so you have four quarters. For each quarter, go over the whole quilt top (and then the quilt back), looking for stray threads and threads caught in seams. For this process, I use a pair of embroidery scissors for clipping short threads, a pair of tweezers for pulling

threads out and a lint roller to collect everything up. You may also wish to press the whole quilt to flatten it out.

Caring for Quilts

If you need to wash your quilt, I always advise washing it on the gentlest cycle you can in order to get it clean and using a mild detergent. If there are both dark and light fabrics in the quilt, I would also throw in a color catcher or two, just in case any of the colors run. You can then dry the quilt on the clothesline or in the tumble dryer on low.

The first time you wash a quilt, the batting will shrink slightly more than the fabrics, which will give the quilt a lovely crinkly, used texture. For this reason, I do not wash my quilts before gifting or selling them because I like them to look brand new. The new owner can have the pleasure of giving the quilt its first wash.

Having said all that, many of my quilts have been washed many times in the machine on a normal cycle with regular strength detergents and come out beautifully. For the first wash, you may want to use a gentle cycle and detergent to be safe.

Into the Light Quilt

Sometimes I have a whole stack of fabric that works together and I like to play around with the stack, taking colors out, adding colors in, arranging the stack in different orders until I come up with something that feels like it could be the basis of a design. Once I arranged the fabrics in this stack from dark to light, it reminded me of the way the sky changes from dark midnight blue, through reds and pinks into the white light of a bright sky. With that idea in mind, I wanted to create a very simple quilt that allowed the colors in each print to really shine and to graduate from dark night to the light of day at the top of the quilt. You will need eighteen different fabrics, organized in value order, so fabric 1 is the lightest and fabric 18 is the darkest.

Finished size
56in (142cm) square approx.

Notes
WOF = width of fabric
FPP = foundation paper piecing
Use ¼in seams, unless otherwise
   instructed

Fabrics used
Quilt top, back and binding: Folk Song
   fabric range by Anna Maria Horner for
   Free Spirit Fabrics

You will need
- Fabrics 1 and 18: one 3¼in (10cm) x WOF strip of each
- Fabrics 2 and 17: one 6½in (20cm) x WOF strip of each
- Fabrics 3 to 16: one 9¾in (25cm) x WOF strip of each
- Backing fabric: 3½yds (3.25m)
- Batting: 64in (162cm) square
- Binding fabric: ½yd (0.5m)
- One copy of Template A and one of Template B (see page 26)
- Two sheets of thin card stock for Templates A and B
- Sixty-four copies of Template C (see page 27)
- Coordinating piecing and quilting threads

CUTTING

1 Using the templates on pages 26–27, photocopy the cutting templates onto thin card stock and cut them out. For Template A, join the two halves at the red lines to make the complete template. I always cut pieces for FPP larger than for regular piecing to give extra all around.

2 Cut eight of Template B from the fabric 1 strip and eight from the fabric 18 strip. Rotate the template 180 degrees along the strip to make the most economical cuts.

3 Cut the fabric 2 and fabric 17 strips into two 3¼in x WOF strips and cut four of Template A from each of these strips (for a total of eight per fabric).

4 Cut the remaining strips (fabrics 3 to 16) into three 3¼in x WOF strips. Cut eight of Template B from one of those strips for each fabric. Cut four of Template A from two of those strips for each fabric (for a total of eight per

fabric). Rotate the template, as before, when making the cuts.

5 From the binding fabric, cut six 2½in x WOF strips.

6 Cut the backing fabric into two equal lengths.

MAKING THE BLOCKS

7 You will need Template C to make each block. The blocks are foundation paper pieced in eight batches of eight to make eight rows of eight identical blocks. The layout in Fig 1 shows which fabrics are placed where in each row of blocks. You will use the Template A shapes for the strips across the center of the blocks and the Template B shapes for the corners. A piecing order has been given by numbers on the templates. Refer to Techniques: Foundation Paper Piecing,

page 16, for full instructions and diagrams on this technique.

8 Place the FPP template wrong side up. Place the section 1 fabric wrong side down on section 1 of Template C so that it covers all of that section plus at least ¼in all around. With right sides together, align and pin the fabric

Fig 1

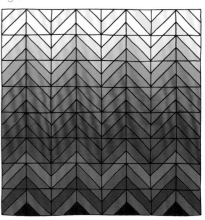

Fig 2

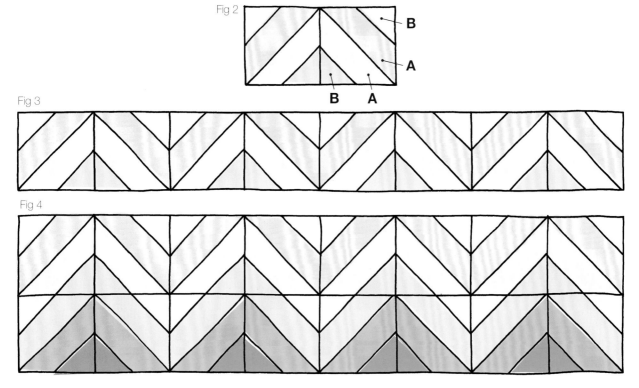

Fig 3

Fig 4

for section 2 so that it will cover all of section 2 plus at least ¼in all around when the seam is sewn and flipped over.

9 Shorten your machine stitch length to 14 to 18 stitches per inch and sew along the seam line between sections 1 and 2 and just beyond that line at each end. Trim the seam allowance to ¼in. Flip the piece over and press flat. Repeat the process with the remaining pieces to complete the sewing of one block.

10 Repeat this process to make sixty-four blocks. Once the blocks are sewn, trim each template and the fabrics along the outer dashed line. Carefully remove the paper.

ASSEMBLING THE QUILT

11 Sew the blocks into pairs, with the darker triangles together (Fig 2).

12 Sew four pairs of blocks together to make each of the eight rows (Fig 3). Press seams in opposite directions in each row so the rows will nest together neatly.

13 Sew the eight rows together so that the colors align. Fig 4 shows how the colors align across two rows.

QUILTING AND FINISHING

14 Sew the two pieces of backing fabric together along the long sides using a ½in seam and press the seam open. Make a quilt sandwich of the quilt back (right side down), the batting and the quilt top (right side up) (see Techniques: Making a Quilt Sandwich, page 18).

15 Quilt as desired. The quilt shown was quilted with horizontal lines approximately 1in apart, using cream thread.

16 When all quilting is finished, square up the quilt, trimming the batting and backing (see Techniques: Squaring Up, page 19).

17 Sew the binding strips together end to end using diagonal seams or straight seams, as preferred. Press wrong sides together all along the length to make a double-fold binding. Bind the quilt to finish, taking care to miter the corners neatly (see Techniques: Making Binding Strips and Binding, pages 19 and 20).

INTO THE LIGHT
Fabric cutting templates
Full size (100%)
Template A: Join Template A at the red lines.

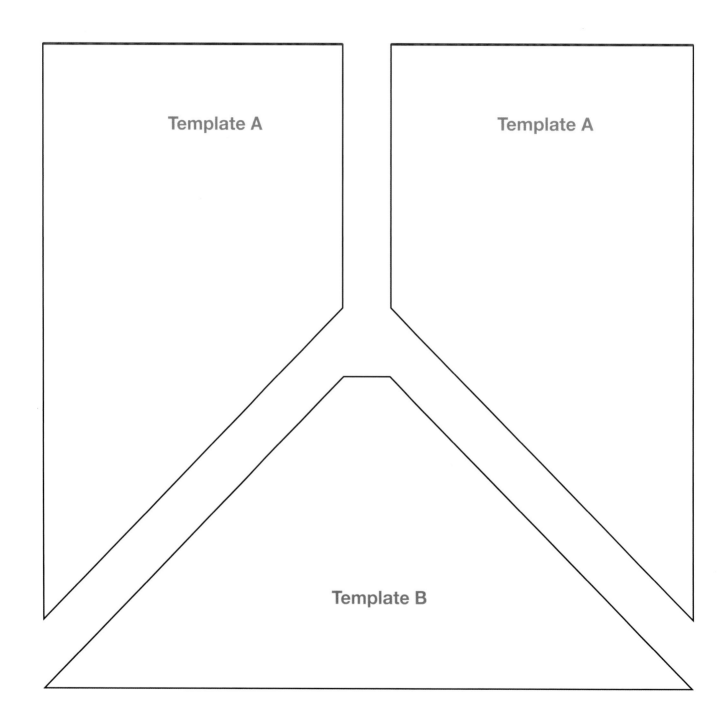

Template A

Template A

Template B

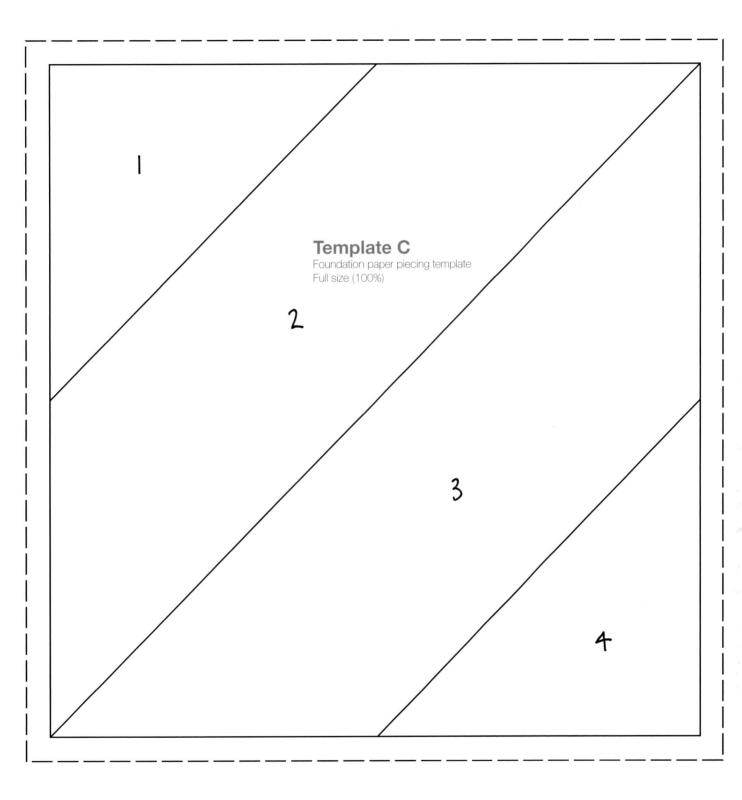

Template C
Foundation paper piecing template
Full size (100%)

1

2

3

4

Birds Migrating Quilt

The idea for this quilt came from simple half-square triangle units. I love how playing around with these in all different layouts can create so many designs. When turned on point, they create a whole new look, and the shapes and patterns made by including some plain squares in with the half-square triangles reminded me of the shapes made in the sky by flocks of birds migrating at the beginning and end of the summer. As I often do with my quilts, I arranged the colors so that they changed gently from dark to light through the quilt, to give the impression that some of the birds were nearer and some further away, flying off into the distance.

Finished size
53in x 70in (135cm x 178cm) approx.

Notes
WOF = width of fabric
F8th = fat eighth (9in x 22in approx.)
HST = half-square triangle
Use ¼in seams, unless otherwise instructed

Fabrics used
Quilt top and binding: Morning Song fabric range by Elizabeth Olwen for Cloud9 Fabrics
Background: Cream Scandi by Makower UK
Quilt back: Tuscany from Va Bene by Dear Stella

You will need
- Seventeen different prints: a F8th of each
- Background fabric: 3yds (2.75m)
- Backing fabric: 4½yds (4m)
- Batting: 61in x 78in (155cm x 200cm)
- Binding fabric: ½yd (0.5m)
- Coordinating piecing and quilting threads

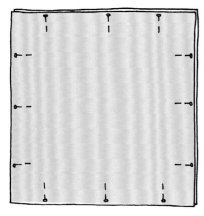

Fig 1A

Fig 1B

Fig 1C

CUTTING

1 From each of the seventeen print F8ths, cut two 7¾in squares (for a total of thirty-four squares).

2 From the background fabric, cut the following:
• Seven 7¾in x WOF strips. Sub-cut each strip into five 7¾in squares to yield thirty-five in total (you will need thirty-four).
• Two 5in x WOF strips. Sub-cut each strip into eight 5in squares to yield sixteen in total (you will need fourteen).
• Three 5½in x WOF strips. Sub-cut each strip into seven 5½in squares to yield twenty-one in total. Cut each in half on the diagonal once, to yield forty-two setting triangles (you will need thirty-six).
• Five 1½in x WOF strips. Sew these strips together end to end for the quilt border, press seams open and set aside for the moment.
• Two 5in x WOF strips. Sew these strips together end to end for the quilt border, press seams open and set aside for the moment.

3 From the binding fabric, cut seven 2½in x WOF strips.

4 Cut the backing fabric into two equal lengths.

MAKING THE BLOCKS

5 Pin one background fabric 7¾in square and one print 7¾in square right sides together (Fig 1A). Sew around all four sides of the square ¼in away from the edge (Fig 1B).

6 Carefully cut the sewn squares along both diagonals, so you have four triangles (Fig 1C).

7 Take each unit, open it up and then press the seam open or to one side and trim off the little triangle points. Trim each HST so it is 5in square. Repeat for all pairs of print and background squares.

ASSEMBLING THE QUILT

8 Sort the HSTs into three piles—dark, medium and light. The dark HSTs will be placed in the bottom third of the quilt, the medium HSTs will be in the middle third and the light HSTs will be in the top third. Lay out all the HSTs, triangles and squares on a floor, table or design wall to decide on the arrangement. Fig 2 shows how each of the rows are assembled, with the positions of the plain squares and the setting triangles. Fig 3 shows the final layout of the blocks.

9 The piecing diagram (Fig 2) shows how to piece the quilt top, in diagonal rows. Seams should be pressed in opposite directions in each row. Trim off the little triangle points after each seam. Finally, trim the corner triangles so that the corners of the quilt are square.

ADDING THE BORDER

10 You can now add the border to your quilt (Fig 4). Measure your quilt across the center width—it should be 51³⁄₈in; if not, make a note of *your* quilt's measurement. Take the very long 1½in wide border strip you sewed earlier and cut a strip to this measurement. Sew this strip to the bottom of the quilt and press the seam outwards. When sewing a border strip to a quilt, match the center of the border to the center point of the quilt and pin. Now pin at either end and then add additional pins in between, easing to fit if necessary. Working in this way will help to avoid wavy edges.

11 Take the very long 5in wide border strip you sewed earlier and cut a strip to fit the width of your quilt. Sew this strip to the top of the quilt and press the seam outwards.

12 Now measure your quilt along the center length—it should be 69⁵⁄₈in; if not, make a note of *your* quilt's measurement. Take the remainder of the very long 1½in wide border strip and cut two strips to this measurement.

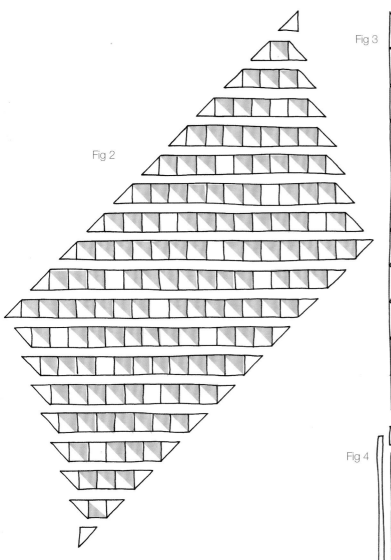

Fig 2

Fig 3

Fig 4

Sew these strips to the sides of the quilt and press seams outwards.

QUILTING AND FINISHING

13 Sew the two pieces of backing fabric together along the long sides using a ½in seam and press the seam open. Make a quilt sandwich of the quilt back (right side down), the batting and the quilt top (right side up) (see Techniques: Making a Quilt Sandwich, page 18).

14 Quilt as desired. The quilt shown was quilted with horizontal lines approximately 1in apart, using cream thread.

15 When all the quilting is finished, square up the quilt, trimming the batting and backing (see Techniques: Squaring Up, page 19).

16 Sew the binding strips together end to end using diagonal seams or straight seams, as preferred. Press wrong sides together all along the length to make a double-fold binding. Bind the quilt to finish, taking care to miter the corners neatly (see Techniques: Making Binding Strips and Binding, pages 19 and 20).

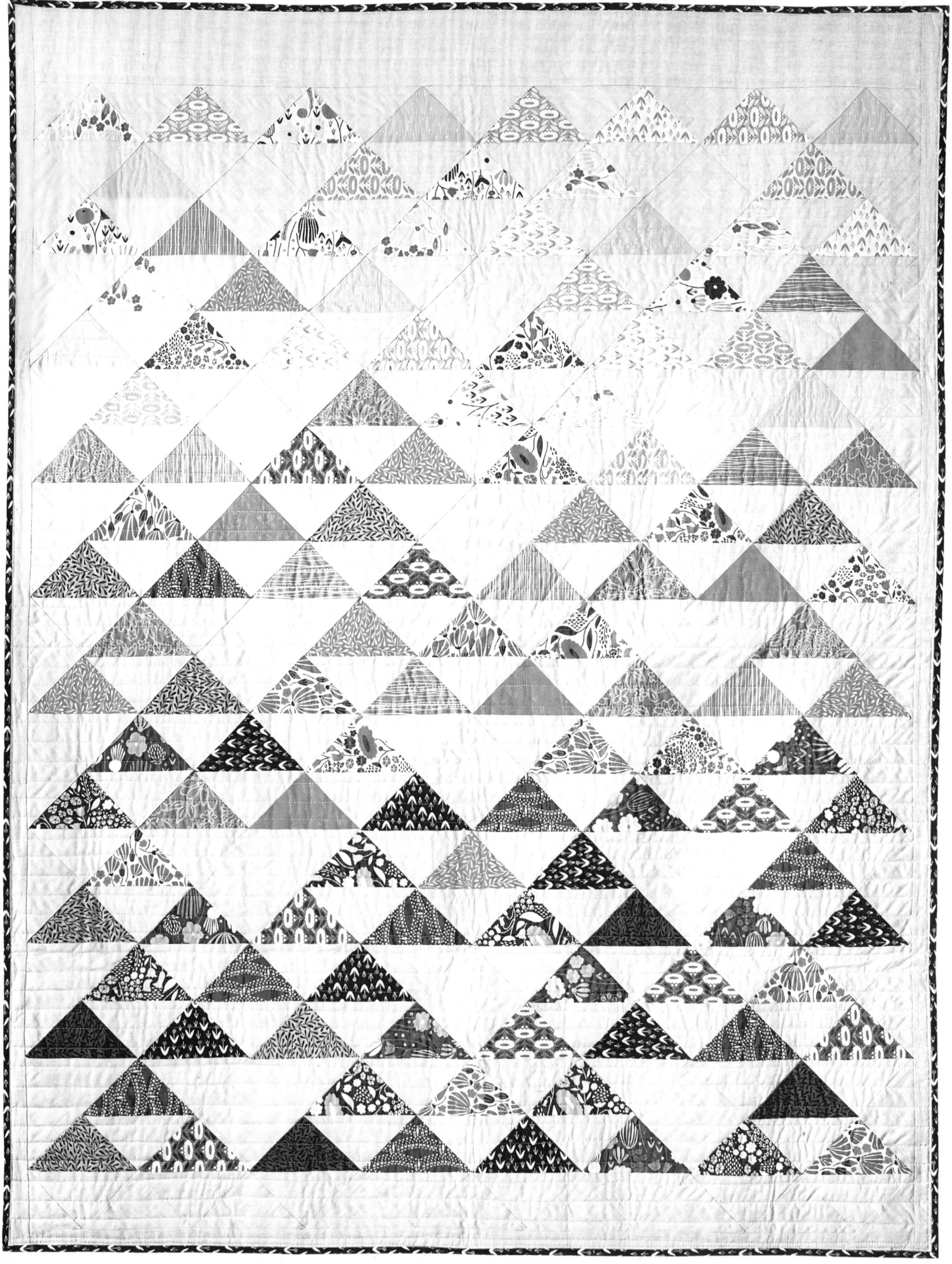

Red Balloon Quilt

This quilt is made of two layers. The first layer is a simple and classic Log Cabin quilt and the second is made up of 2in squares pieced together and then cut out to make a red balloon in appliqué. I always loved the French film *Le Ballon Rouge*, and how everything in that film was in black and white except for the balloon itself. This quilt was designed to reflect the simplicity of the photography in that film.

Finished size
52½in (135cm) square approx.

Notes
F8th = fat eighth (9in x 22in approx.)
FQ = fat quarter
Use ¼in seams, unless instructed otherwise

Fabrics used
Quilt top and binding: Modern Backgrounds by Zen Chic for Moda fabrics with assorted reds from my own stash for the balloon
Quilt back: Quilt Back by Whistler Studios for Windham Fabrics

You will need
- Grey fabric: one 9in (25cm) square
- Cream and white fabrics: twenty-two F8ths (also used for binding)
- Light red fabric: three 2½in (6.5cm) squares
- Medium red fabric: fifty-one 2½in (6.5cm) squares
- Medium-dark red fabric: twelve 2½in (6.5cm) squares
- Dark red fabric: six 2½in (6.5cm) squares
- Balloon "string" fabric: one FQ
- Backing fabric: 3½yds (3m)
- Batting: 60in (155cm) square
- Fusible web: 20in (50cm) strip of 18in (46cm) wide
- One copy each of templates A, B, C and D (see pages 38–39)
- Coordinating piecing and quilting threads
- Bias tape maker (optional)

Fig 1

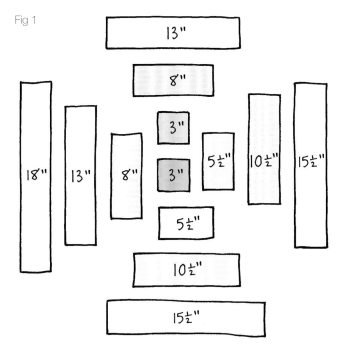

Fig 2

CUTTING

1 Cut the grey 9in square into nine 3in squares, for the center of the Log Cabin blocks.

2 Cut each of the twenty-two cream and white fabric F8ths into three 3in x 22in strips. Sub-cut the strips as follows (you will have some strips left over for the binding):
• Cut each of nine strips into one 3in and one 18in length.
• Cut each of eighteen strips into one 5½in and one 15½in length.
• Cut each of eighteen strips into one 8in and one 13in length.
• Cut each of nine strips into two lengths of 10½in.

3 Trim the remaining strips of cream and white fabrics into 2½in strips to be used for the binding.

4 Cut two 1in wide bias strips from the balloon "string" fabric FQ. Cutting it on the bias will allow you to curve the fabric strip slightly.

5 Cut the backing fabric into two equal lengths.

MAKING THE BLOCKS

6 Sew each of the nine Log Cabin blocks in the same way, as follows. Start with the grey 3in center square and add cream and white strips around it, starting with the shortest lengths and working up to the longest, working clockwise with the strips shown in Fig 1. Press seams away from the center after each new piece is added. Add the strips in the

following order: 3in, 5½in, 5½in, 8in, 8in, 10½in, 10½in, 13in, 13in, 15½in, 15½in, 18in. When the block is made, check that it is 18in square.

7 When all nine Log Cabin blocks are made, sew them into three rows each with three blocks. Press seams in opposite directions in each row. Sew the three rows together and press seams.

MAKING THE BALLOON

8 Sew the seventy-two red 2½in squares together in an 8 x 9 layout, in the order shown in Fig 2, where L = light, M = medium, MD = medium dark and D = dark. Sew the squares into rows first, pressing seams in opposite directions in each row, then sew the rows together. Press seams as preferred.

9 Cut out the four balloon templates (A, B, C and D) and tape together as shown in Fig 3. Trace the complete balloon shape onto the back of the fusible web and cut out. Note: Remember that the image will be reversed when you lay it out on the quilt.

10 Fuse the fusible web balloon shape to the back of the red squares piece, placing the shape at an angle and making sure that the lighter squares sit in the A section of the template and the darker squares in the D section of the template. Cut out the balloon shape neatly. Peel off the backing paper and fuse the balloon to the quilt (see quilt photo). Topstitch, zigzag-stitch or blanket-stitch around the edge of the appliqué to secure.

11 Sew the two bias-cut strips of string fabric together end to end and press the seam open. Create a ½in bias tape by folding the outside edges to the center and pressing. If you have one, a bias tape maker is a useful tool for this job.

12 Pin the balloon string onto the quilt (see photo for position) and hand- or machine-stitch it in place to finish the quilt top.

QUILTING AND FINISHING

13 Sew the two pieces of backing fabric together along the long sides using a ½in seam and press the seam open. Make a quilt sandwich of the quilt back (right side down), the batting and the quilt top (right side up) (see Techniques: Making a Quilt Sandwich, page 18).

14 Quilt as desired. The quilt shown was quilted with horizontal lines approximately ½in apart in cream thread.

15 When all quilting is finished, square up the quilt, trimming the batting and backing (see Techniques: Squaring Up, page 19).

16 Sew the remaining strips of cream and white fabrics together for the binding, sewing the strips end to end using diagonal seams or straight seams, as preferred—you will need a sewn length of about 220in. Press wrong sides together all along the length to make a double-fold binding. Bind the quilt to finish, taking care to miter the corners neatly (see Techniques: Making Binding Strips and Binding, pages 19 and 20).

Fig 3

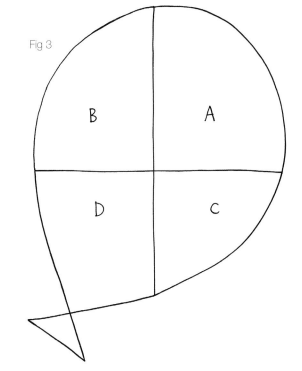

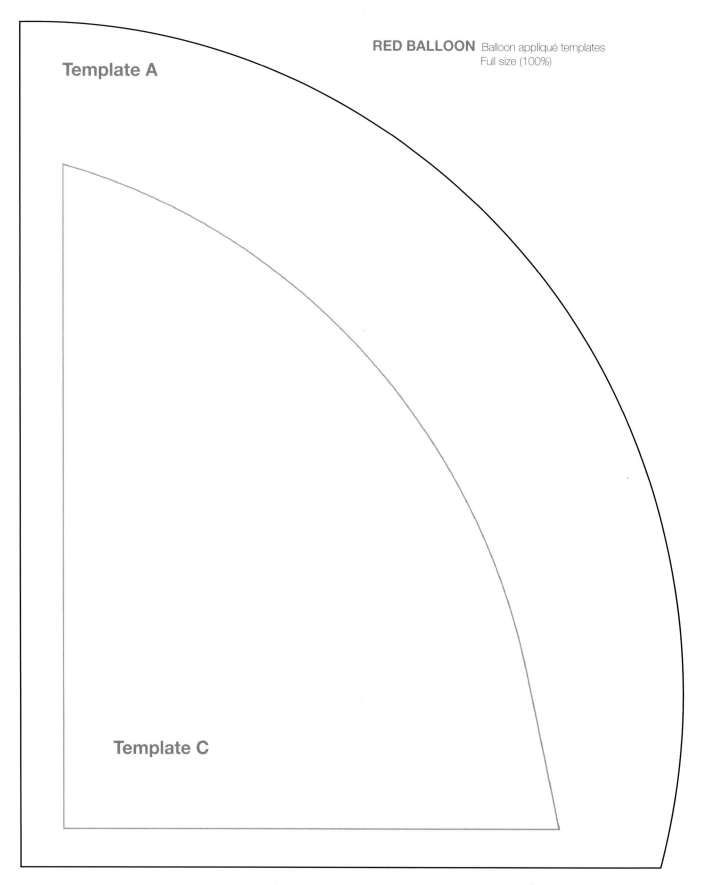

Template A

Template C

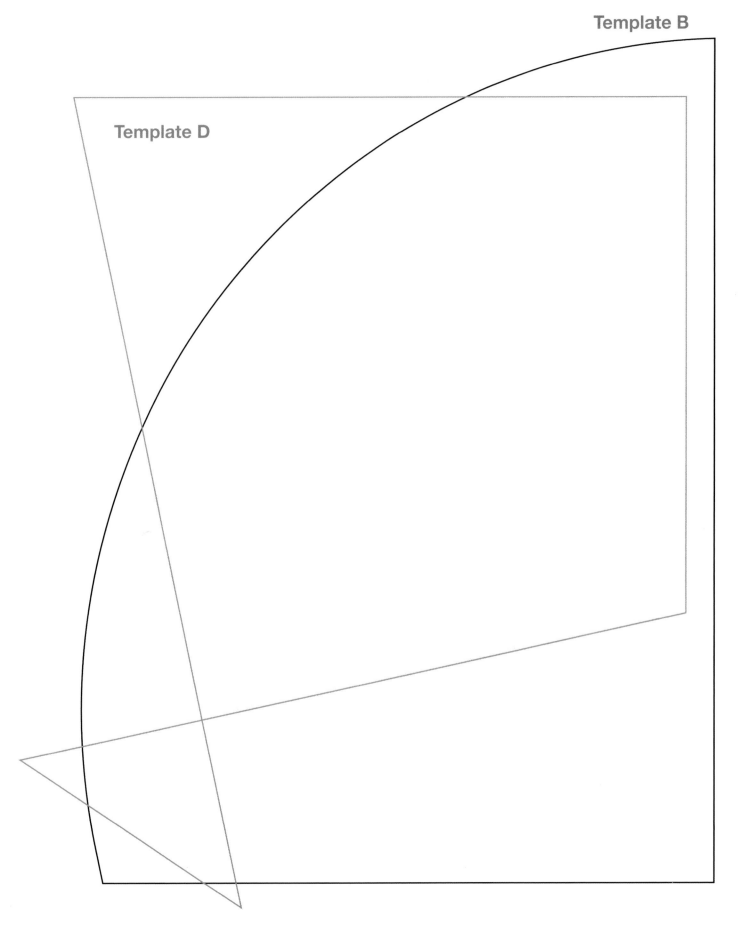

Template B

Template D

Supernova Quilt

The lone star is a classic quilt block, and no wonder as it makes such a dramatic statement. This version uses fewer, larger diamonds than most lone star quilts for a quicker and easier finish. When choosing and cutting the fabrics, refer to Fig 1 for the placement of each fabric. Fabric 1 is the darkest black/white print, grading up to Fabric 9 for the lightest. Fabric 5 is the background color—I used a peachy-orange for contrast.

Finished size
60in (152cm) square approx.

Notes
WOF = width of fabric
Use ¼in seams, unless otherwise instructed

Fabrics used
Quilt top: Black and White by Cotton + Steel and Tropicana from RJR Supreme Solids
Quilt back: Black from RJR Supreme Solids
Binding: Tropicana from RJR Supreme Solids

You will need
- Fabric 1 (darkest black/white) and Fabric 9 (lightest black/white) for star: 3in (10cm) x WOF strip of each
- Fabrics 2 and 8 (black/white) for star: 6in (20cm) x WOF strip of each
- Fabrics 3 and 7 (black/white) for star: 9in (30cm) x WOF strip of each
- Fabrics 4 and 6 (black/white) for star: 12in (40cm) x WOF strip of each
- Background fabric (Fabric 5): 2½yds (2.25m)
- Backing fabric: 3¾yds (3.5m)
- Batting: 68in (175cm) square
- Binding fabric: ½yd (0.5m)—I used the same fabric as the background
- Coordinating piecing and quilting threads

Fig 1

CUTTING

1 Fig 1 shows the lone star layout, identifying the fabrics used. From the black/white lone star fabrics, cut the following WOF strips:

- Fabrics 1 and 9: one 3in x WOF strip.
- Fabrics 2 and 8: two 3in x WOF strips.
- Fabrics 3 and 7: three 3in x WOF strips.
- Fabrics 4 and 6: four 3in x WOF strips.

2 From the background fabric (Fabric 5), cut the following:
- Five 3in x WOF strips.
- Two 15in x WOF strips. Cut each of these strips into two 15in squares and then cut them in half along one diagonal to make eight triangles in total.
- Two 20in x WOF strips. Cut each of these strips into two 20in squares and then cut them in half along one diagonal to make eight triangles in total.

3 From the binding fabric, cut seven 2½in x WOF strips.

4 Cut the backing fabric into two equal lengths.

MAKING THE QUILT UNITS

5 Sew the 3in strips into the following groups of strips, staggering the ends of the strips as in Fig 2. Staggering the ends by about 2½in should be sufficient. Press seams open or to one side, as preferred.

- 1, 2, 3, 4, background.
- 2, 3, 4, background, 6.
- 3, 4, background, 6, 7.
- 4, background, 6, 7, 8.
- Background, 6, 7, 8, 9.

6 Cut each set of strips into eight diagonal strips as shown in Fig 3. To do this, align the sets of strips with the horizontal

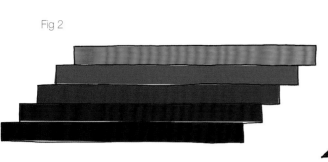

Fig 2

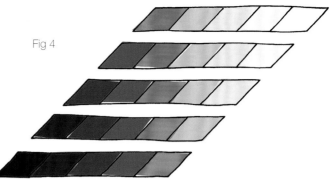

Fig 4

Fig 3

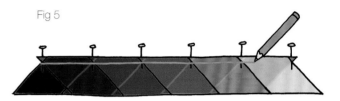

Fig 5

Fig 6

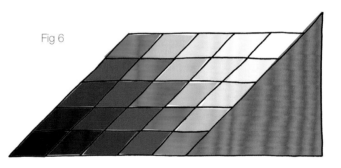

lines on your cutting mat, then cut 3in wide strips at a 45-degree angle. You will have eight pieced segments, each with five diamond colors.

7 Take one pieced segment from each of the five sets and sew them together following the layout in Fig 4. To do this, mark a ¼in line along the side of one of the pieces to be joined, on the wrong side of the fabric. Pin the two strips of fabric together so that the seams meet at the ¼in line and then pin each intersection (Fig 5). Press seams open or to one side, as preferred.

8 Divide the eight finished diamonds into two piles, A and B—this will create the two halves of the star. Using the diamonds from the A pile, take one diamond and sew a 15in triangle to the side as shown in Fig 6, so that the point of the triangle extends beyond the point of the diamond, but is aligned along the bottom. Press seams towards the triangle. Trim the top of the triangle (Fig 7).

Fig 7

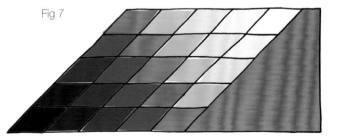

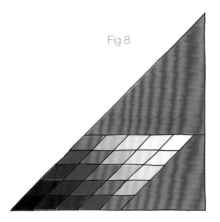

Fig 8

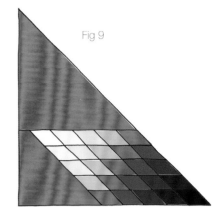

Fig 9

9 Sew a 20in triangle to the other side of the diamond, aligning it as shown in Fig 8. Press seams towards the triangle. Repeat this process with the other diamonds from the A pile to make four of these A sections in total.

10 Now use the diamonds from the B pile and make four B sections using the same process but with the triangles attached to the opposite sides, as shown in Fig 9.

ASSEMBLING THE QUILT

11 Sew the A and B sections into pairs along the diagonal to make four squares. Press seams open or to one side, as preferred (Fig 10).

12 Sew the four squares into two pairs and press seams open or to one side, as preferred.

13 Now sew the two halves of the quilt together and press seams open or to one side, as preferred. Trim the quilt to 60½in square.

QUILTING AND FINISHING

14 Sew the two pieces of backing fabric together along the long sides using a ½in seam and press the seam open. Make a quilt sandwich of the quilt back (right side down), the batting and the quilt top (right side up) (see Techniques: Making a Quilt Sandwich, page 18).

15 Quilt as desired. The quilt shown was quilted with a pale thread in a diagonal crosshatch pattern of lines 1¼in apart, set ⅝in away from the main diagonal seam lines.

16 When quilting is finished, square up the quilt, trimming the batting and backing (see Techniques: Squaring Up, page 19).

17 Sew the binding strips together end to end using diagonal seams or straight seams, as preferred. Press wrong sides together all along the length to make a double-fold binding. Bind the quilt to finish, taking care to miter the corners neatly (see Techniques: Making Binding Strips and Binding, pages 19 and 20).

Fig 10

Summer Picnic Blanket

This attractive quilt is perfect for long, lazy summer picnics. It is also a great stash buster, as you can use a whole heap of scraps or a selection of fat quarters. The important thing is to divide the fabrics into light and dark. The fabrics I used in this quilt are all from the Kaffe Fassett Collective, known for rich patterns and colors. The saturated blues and purples contrast with the softer mauves and greys to reflect the warm colors of summer.

Finished size
65in (165cm) square approx.

Notes
WOF = width of fabric
FQ = fat quarter
Use ¼in seams, unless instructed otherwise

Fabrics used
Quilt top: Kaffe Fassett Collective by Westminster Fibers
Quilt back: Botanique by Joel Dewberry for Westminster Fibers
Binding: Flurry by Dashwood Studio

You will need
- Twelve dark FQs, or the equivalent in scraps (if the FQs are 22in wide throughout, only nine will be needed)
- Seven light FQs, or the equivalent in scraps
- Frixion Erasable Marker Pen
- Backing fabric: 4yds (3.75m)
- Batting: 73in (185cm) square
- Binding fabric: ½yd (0.5m)
- Coordinating piecing and quilting threads, such as 50wt Aurifil 1240 (dark maroon) and 2600 (dove)

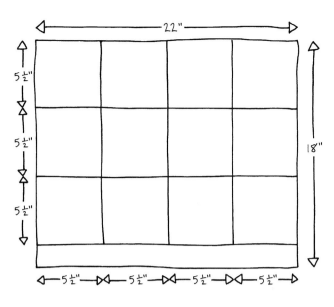

Fig 1
Cut three strips 5½in x 22in.
Sub-cut each strip into three 5½in squares (or four if FQ is wide enough).

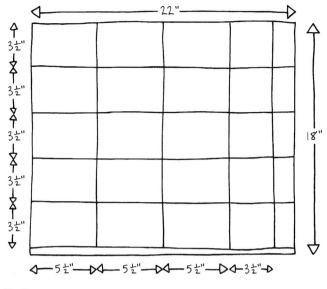

Fig 2
Cut five strips 3½in x 22in.
Sub-cut each strip into three 3½in x 5½in rectangles and one 3½in square.

CUTTING

1 Cut each of the twelve (or nine, if using 22in wide FQ) dark FQs into three 5½in x 22in strips. Sub-cut each of these strips into three (or four if your FQs are big enough) 5½in squares (see Fig 1). You will need 100 in total.

2 Cut each of the seven light FQs into five 3½in x 22in strips. Sub-cut each of these strips into three 3½in x 5½in rectangles and one 3½in square (see Fig 2). You will need 100 rectangles and twenty-five squares in total.

3 From the binding fabric, cut seven 2½in x WOF strips.

4 Cut the backing fabric into two equal lengths.

MAKING THE BLOCKS

5 Sew two dark 5½in squares to either side of one light 3½in x 5½in rectangle. Press seams towards the dark fabrics (Fig 3). This is Unit A. Repeat to make fifty of these units in total.

6 Sew two light 3½in x 5½in rectangles to either side of one different light 3½in square. Press seams towards the center square (Fig 4). This is Unit B. Repeat to make twenty-five of these units in total.

7 Sew two of Unit A to either side of one Unit B, taking care to align seams. Press seams towards the center strip (Fig 5). This is one block—Unit C. The block should measure 13½in square. Repeat to make twenty-five units in total. To help with the final layout, place a pin in the center of each block, parallel with the seams just pressed inwards (Fig 6).

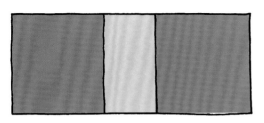

Fig 3
Unit A

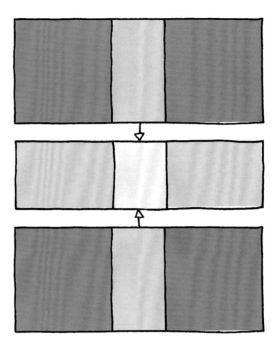

Fig 5

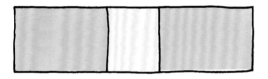

Fig 4
Unit B

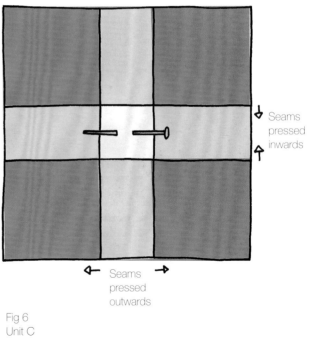

Seams
pressed
inwards

← Seams →
pressed
outwards

Fig 6
Unit C
Place pin parallel to seams pressed
inwards.

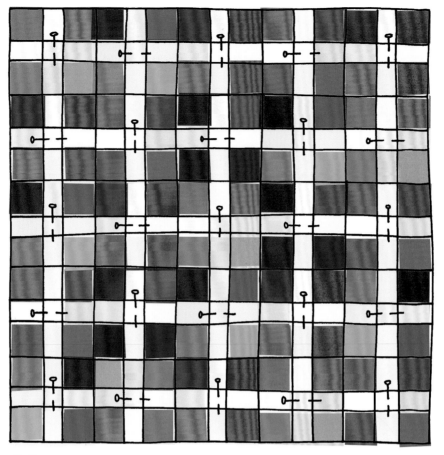

Fig 7

ASSEMBLING THE QUILT

8 To assemble the quilt top, arrange the twenty-five blocks on a design wall (or table, floor or bed) to decide on the best layout. Note: so that all seams on all blocks nest with those on adjacent blocks, rotate each block so that the pins are always facing in a different direction from those on the adjacent blocks (Fig 7). The blocks can then be numbered. I numbered mine in rows using a Frixion pen (you could use any erasable marker), so the first row is blocks A1, A2, A3, A4 and A5, the second row is blocks B1, B2, B3, B4 and B5, and so on.

9 Sew the blocks into five rows, each with five blocks. Press the row seams in opposite directions.

10 Sew the five rows together to finish the quilt top. Press the seams open or to one side as desired.

QUILTING AND FINISHING

11 Sew the two pieces of backing fabric together along the long sides using a ½in seam and press the seam open. Make a quilt sandwich of the quilt back (right side down), the batting and the quilt top (right side up) (see Techniques: Making a Quilt Sandwich, page 18).

12 Quilt as desired. The quilt shown was quilted in a grid of vertical and horizontal lines 1in apart, set ½in away from each seam line. The quilting threads used were 50wt Aurifil 1240 (dark maroon) across the darker stripes in the quilt and 2600 (dove) across the lighter.

13 When quilting is finished, square up the quilt, trimming the batting and backing (see Techniques: Squaring Up, page 19).

14 Sew the binding strips together end to end using diagonal seams or straight seams, as preferred. Press wrong sides together all along the length to make a double-fold binding. Bind the quilt to finish, taking care to miter the corners neatly (see Techniques: Making Binding Strips and Binding, pages 19 and 20).

Under My Umbrella Quilt

The circus stripe prints in this fabric line by Tula Pink immediately made me think of a whole selection of brightly colored beach umbrellas, and I imagined the faces in the prints peeking out from under the umbrellas. Any striped fabrics could be used to make this quilt, mixed with a variety of prints for the background. Here, I have alternated warm colors with cool colors, to provide contrast between the blocks.

Finished size
60in (152cm) square approx.

Notes
LOF = length of fabric
FQ = fat quarter
WOF = width of fabric
Use ¼in seams, unless instructed
  otherwise

Fabrics used
Quilt top, back and binding: Elizabeth
  fabric range by Tula Pink for
  Free Spirit Fabrics

You will need
- For the umbrellas: ¾yd (0.75m) of each of four fabrics
- For the backgrounds: one FQ of each of sixteen
  fabrics
- Backing fabric: 3¾yds (3.5m)
- Batting: 68in (175cm) square
- Binding fabric: ½yd (0.5m)
- One copy of the triangle template (see page 56)
- Coordinating piecing and quilting threads

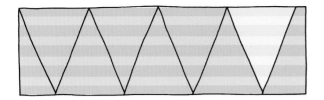

Fig 1

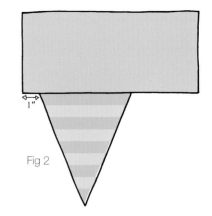

Fig 2

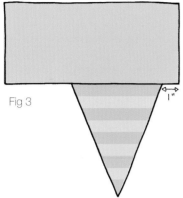

Fig 3

Fig 4

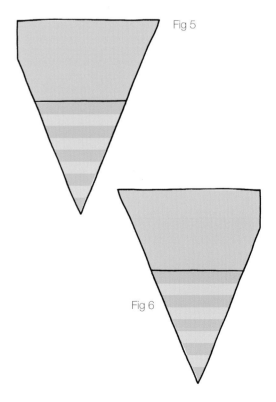

Fig 5

Fig 6

CUTTING

1 From each of the four umbrella fabrics, cut five 7in wide x LOF strips, cutting so the stripe on each fabric is positioned identically for each triangle, and the stripes are also perfectly horizontal on each triangle. Using the template as a guide, sub-cut each strip into seven triangles, rotating the template 180 degrees on alternate cuts, as shown in Fig 1. This will give you thirty-five triangles per color (you need thirty-two of each). Arrange the triangles in piles of the same fabric color.

2 From each of the sixteen background fabrics, cut two 4½in x WOF strips. Sub-cut each of these strips into four 4½in x 10in rectangles (to yield eight rectangles from each background fabric—128 in total).

3 From the binding fabric, cut six 2½in x WOF strips.

4 Cut the backing fabric into two equal lengths.

MAKING A BLOCK

5 Take one pile of eight triangles of the same print. Sew four rectangles of one background print to the top of four of the triangles, with the rectangles offset by approximately 1in at one end, as in Fig 2.

6 Sew four rectangles of another background print to the top of the remaining four triangles, with the rectangles offset by approximately 1in at the other end, as in Fig 3. Press

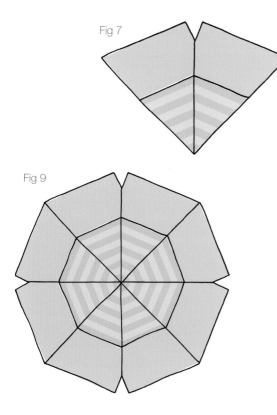

Fig 7

Fig 8

Fig 9

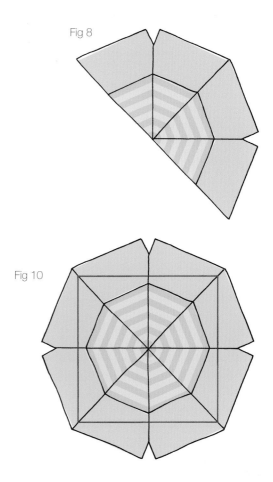

Fig 10

the seams of one set of four towards the triangles and the seams of the other set towards the rectangles.

7 Trim off excess fabric using the 45-degree line on your cutting mat (Fig 4). You will now have four triangle/rectangle units as in Fig 5 and four as in Fig 6.

8 Assemble a block using these eight sewn units, sewing the units into pairs along the shorter diagonals (Fig 7). Now sew two pairs together as shown in Fig 8. Press seams open or to one side, as preferred.

9 Sew the two halves of the block together (Fig 9). Press seams open or to one side, as preferred. Trim the block to 15½in square (Fig 10).

10 Repeat this process to make fifteen more blocks, for a total of sixteen blocks.

ASSEMBLING THE QUILT

11 Lay out the sixteen blocks in a pleasing manner; this quilt features colors in diagonal rows. Sew the blocks into four rows each with four blocks, pressing seams in opposite directions in each row.

12 Sew the four rows together to finish the quilt top.

QUILTING AND FINISHING

13 Sew the two pieces of backing fabric together along the long sides using a ½in seam and press the seam open. Make a quilt sandwich of the quilt back (right side down), the batting and the quilt top (right side up) (see Techniques: Making a Quilt Sandwich, page 18).

14 Quilt as desired. The quilt shown was quilted in a diagonal crosshatch pattern of wavy lines approximately 2in apart, using pale thread.

15 When quilting is finished, square up the quilt, trimming the batting and backing (see Techniques: Squaring Up, page 19).

16 Sew the binding strips together end to end using diagonal seams or straight seams, as preferred. Press wrong sides together all along the length to make a double-fold binding. Bind the quilt to finish, taking care to miter the corners neatly (see Techniques: Making Binding Strips and Binding, pages 19 and 20).

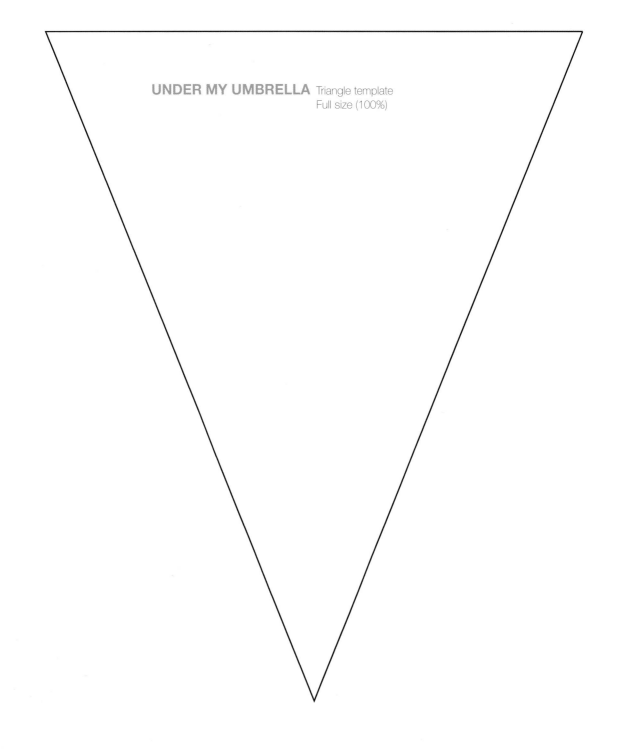

UNDER MY UMBRELLA Triangle template
Full size (100%)

Kodachrome Quilt

I've always loved the contrast between blacks, whites and greys and bright colors. When I started putting this quilt together and creating the colored and grey-scale blocks, it reminded me of growing up and taking black and white photos because they were cheaper to develop than color film—not a problem we have any more! This colorful quilt is great for using up all those leftover "layer cake" slices (10in squares) you may have lying around. Cutting stacks of squares and strip piecing make this quilt quick and easy to make.

Finished size
64in (163cm) square approx.

Notes
WOF = width of fabric
Use ¼in seams, unless instructed otherwise

Fabrics used
Quilt top: Layer Cakes® from various Moda fabric lines, including Modern Backgrounds by Zen Chic
Backing: Check from Pam Kitty Picnic by Pam Vieira-McGinnis for Lakehouse Fabrics
Binding: White on black dot by Makower UK

You will need
- Thirty-two colored 10in (25.5cm) squares
- Sixteen cream/white 10in (25.5cm) squares
- Eight black 10in (25.5cm) squares
- Eight grey 10in (25.5cm) squares
- Backing fabric: 4yds (3.75m)
- Batting: 72in (185cm) square
- Binding fabric: ½yd (0.5m)
- Coordinating piecing and quilting threads

CUTTING

1 If using 10in squares from layer cakes, trim them to exactly 10in square because sometimes they are slightly larger.

2 Cut each of the 10in squares into four 2½in x 10in strips. You can speed up the process by cutting up to eight squares in one cut; be sure your rotary cutter blade is very sharp.

3 Cut the binding fabric into seven 2½in x WOF strips.

4 Cut the backing fabric into two equal lengths.

MAKING THE BLOCKS

5 There are sixty-four blocks in the quilt, each one made as a sixteen-patch block using strip piecing. To make one block, start by picking two sets of 2½in x 10in color fabric strips—one darker and one lighter. Sew them into two groups of four along the long sides, alternating dark/light/dark/light (Fig 1). Press seams towards the darker fabrics.

6 Cut across the seams so you have four 2½in x 10in strips (Fig 2).

7 Alternating the colors, sew the strips back together into 8½in squares (Fig 3). Press seams open or to one side, as preferred. This makes one block.

8 Repeat this process to make the rest of the blocks, pairing all the colored squares, and then pairing cream with grey and then pairing cream with black. When all of the blocks are sewn, you should have thirty-two colored blocks, sixteen cream/grey blocks and sixteen cream/black blocks.

ASSEMBLING THE QUILT

9 Lay out the blocks so the colored blocks alternate with cream/black blocks and cream/grey blocks. Sew the blocks into eight rows each with eight blocks. Press the seams in opposite directions in each row.

10 Sew the eight rows together to finish the quilt top. Press the seams open or to one side, as preferred.

QUILTING AND FINISHING

11 Sew the two pieces of backing fabric together along the long sides using a ½in seam and press the seam open. Make a quilt sandwich of the quilt back (right side down), the batting and the quilt top (right side up) (see Techniques: Making a Quilt Sandwich, page 18).

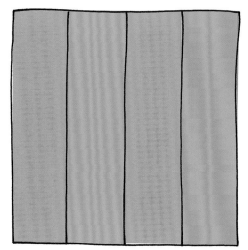

Fig 1

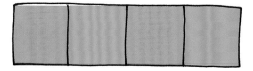

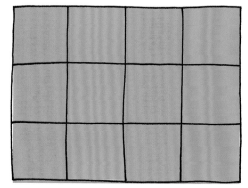

Fig 2

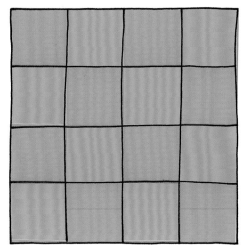

Fig 3

12 Quilt as desired. For the quilt shown, a hera marker was used to mark a diagonal crosshatch pattern of lines 1in apart, set ½in away from each seam line. The quilt shown was quilted using pale thread.

13 When quilting is finished, square up the quilt, trimming the batting and backing (see Techniques: Squaring Up, page 19).

14 Sew the binding strips together end to end using diagonal seams or straight seams, as preferred. Press wrong sides together all along the length to make a double-fold binding. Bind the quilt to finish, taking care to miter the corners neatly (see Techniques: Making Binding Strips and Binding, pages 19 and 20).

Sparkling Diamonds Quilt

When I design a quilt, the idea often comes from the fabric line. This line has a series of simple, strong-colored prints and I wanted to come up with a design that really showed off those big, bold colors. Grading the colors from light in the center to darker at the edges of the quilt creates a pattern that radiates out across the quilt. Each block is paper pieced, but the process is very quick because there is only one seam per block. For anyone who hasn't tried foundation paper piecing before, this quilt is a great place to start.

Finished size
63in x 84in (160cm x 213cm) approx.

Notes
WOF = width of fabric
FQ = fat quarter
Use ¼in seams, unless otherwise
 instructed

Fabrics used
Quilt top: Pie Making Day by Brenda
 Ratliff for RJR Fabrics, mixed with a
 variety of black and white blenders
Quilt back: Comma by Zen for Moda
 Fabrics

You will need
- Orange prints: four FQs
- Yellow prints: four FQs
- Lime green prints: four FQs
- Teal prints: four FQs
- Cerise prints: four FQs
- Black/white prints: seventeen FQs
- Backing fabric: 5¼yds (4.8m)
- Batting: 71in x 92in (180cm x 235cm)
- Binding fabric: ³⁄₈yd (0.3m)
- One hundred and ninety-six templates—make ninety-eight of each shown on page 67
- Coordinating piecing and quilting threads

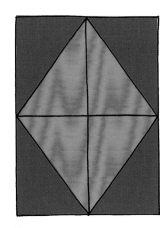

Fig 1A

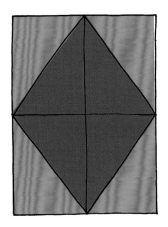

Fig 1B

CUTTING

1 From each orange FQ, cut three 6in x 8in rectangles, to create twelve in total.

2 From each yellow FQ, cut four 6in x 8in rectangles, to create sixteen in total.

3 From each lime green, teal and cerise FQ, cut six 6in x 8in rectangles, to create twenty-four of each color in total.

4 From each black/white FQ, cut six 6in x 8in rectangles, to create 102 in total.

5 Cut half of the rectangles of each color in half along the diagonal from top left to bottom right. Cut the other half of the rectangles of each color in half along the diagonal from top right to bottom left.

6 From the binding fabric, cut eight 2½in x WOF strips.

7 Cut the backing fabric into two equal lengths.

MAKING THE HALF-RECTANGLE BLOCKS

8 The half-rectangle blocks are created using foundation paper piecing, with color prints on one half of each template and the black/white prints on the other. Refer to Techniques: Foundation Paper Piecing, page 16, for full instructions and diagrams on this technique. The basic process for this quilt is as follows. Take a color triangle and place it on the back of the template over one of the triangles, with the right side of the fabric facing up. It should cover the paper triangle with at least ¼in overlap around all edges. Pin in place. Take a black/white triangle and place it right sides together with the

color triangle, aligning the long diagonal edge. Pin in place. Turn the template over to the printed side and sew along the diagonal line, going a little past the line at each end.

9 Press the seam and then fold the template out of the way to trim the seam allowance to ¼in. Fold the template back in place and trim the template to size along the outer dashed lines. Remove the paper from the block.

10 Use this process to paper piece the rest of the half-rectangle blocks. You need 196 in total.

ASSEMBLING THE DIAMOND BLOCKS

11 Sew the blocks into groups of four to make the diamonds in the quilt. Do this by first sewing two pairs of triangles together and pressing the seams in opposite directions in each row of the block. Then sew those two pieces together to make each diamond block. Take care to mix fabrics up so that the same fabrics do not sit next to one another. Make the diamond blocks as follows (see Fig 1A and 1B).
* One orange block with orange in the center.
* Four orange blocks with black in the center.
* Eight yellow blocks with yellow in the center.
* Twelve lime green blocks with black in the center.
* Twelve teal blocks with teal in the center.
* Eight cerise blocks with black in the center.
* Four cerise blocks with cerise in the center.

12 Each diamond block should measure 9½in x 12½in. Once the blocks are made, sew them into seven rows, each with seven blocks (see Fig 2). Press seams in opposite directions in each row. Sew the seven rows together to finish the quilt top.

Fig 2

QUILTING AND FINISHING

13 Sew the two pieces of backing fabric together along the long sides using a ½in seam and press the seam open. Make a quilt sandwich of the quilt back (right side down), the batting and the quilt top (right side up) (see Techniques: Making a Quilt Sandwich, page 18).

14 Quilt as desired. The quilt shown was quilted with a diagonal crosshatch pattern of lines about 2in apart, using cream thread.

15 When quilting is finished, square up the quilt, trimming the batting and backing (see Techniques: Squaring Up, page 19).

16 Sew the binding strips together end to end using diagonal seams or straight seams, as preferred. Press wrong sides together all along the length to make a double-fold binding. Bind the quilt to finish, taking care to miter the corners neatly (see Techniques: Making Binding Strips and Binding, pages 19 and 20).

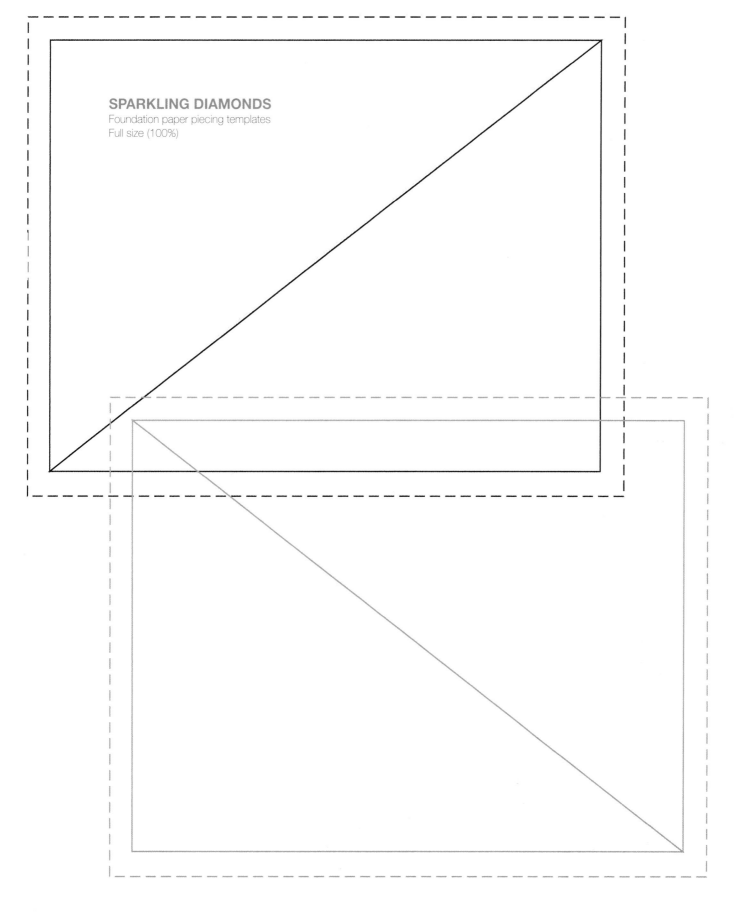

SPARKLING DIAMONDS
Foundation paper piecing templates
Full size (100%)

Scrappy Trees Quilt

This fresh and modern quilt was pieced using a method called quilt as you go (QAYG). For this method, each block is quilted and the blocks are then joined into the quilt using joining strips. The advantages of using this method are that it is much easier to quilt the blocks on a home sewing machine and the trees can be appliquéd on top of the quilting without having to manipulate a whole quilt. I am indebted to Marianne Haak of thequiltingedge.com for her tutorials on this method.

Finished size
70in (178cm) square approx.

Notes
QAYG = quilt as you go
LOF = length of fabric
WOF = width of fabric
Use ¼in seams, unless instructed otherwise

Fabrics used
Quilt top: Squared Elements by Art Gallery Fabrics for the background, Robert Kaufman Kona solids for the joining strips and binding, and scraps of various fabrics for the trees
Quilt back: Yuwa Live Life Collection

You will need
- Background fabric: 3¾yds (3.5m)
- Trees: lots of small scraps
- Joining strips front: ¾yd (0.7m)
- Joining strips back: 1yd (0.9m)
- Backing fabric: 4¾yds (4.5m)
- Batting: 2½yds (2.25m) of 90in (230cm) wide
- Binding fabric: ½yd (0.5m)
- Dishes, bowls or dinner plates: approx. 5in (12.5cm), 10in (25.5cm) and 15in (38cm) diameter
- Fusible web: 2½yds (2.25m) of 18in (46cm) wide
- Binding clips (such as Clover Wonder Clips)
- Coordinating piecing and quilting threads

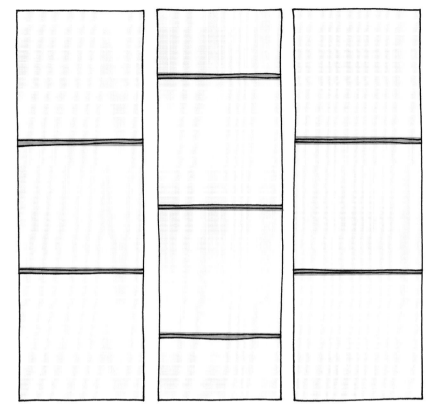

Fig 1

CUTTING

1 From the background fabric, cut a 54in long LOF piece. Cut this into five 8in x 54in LOF strips. Reserve four of these strips for the border. From the fifth strip cut four 8in squares (for the border corners) and discard the remainder of the strip.

2 Cut the remainder of the background fabric into eight 18in squares and two 9in x 18in rectangles.

3 From the backing fabric, cut a 58in long LOF piece. Cut this into four 11in x 58in LOF strips (for the border). If your usable fabric width is only 42in wide, then you can cut these at 10½in rather than 11in.

4 Cut the remainder of the backing fabric into eight 22in squares, two 13in x 22in rectangles and four 11in squares (for the border corners). If your fabric width is 42in rather than 44in, these pieces can be cut to 10½in and 21in wide instead of 11in and 22in.

5 Cut the batting into the following pieces:
• Four 11in x 58in strips (for the border).
• Eight 22in squares.
• Two 13in x 22in rectangles.
• Four 11in squares (for the border corners).

6 Cut the front joining strips into fourteen 1¾in x WOF strips and sub-cut as follows:
• Cut five strips into seven 18in lengths and four 8in lengths.
• Sew the remaining nine x WOF strips end to end and cut into four 54in and two 70in lengths.

7 Cut the back joining strips into fourteen 2¼in x WOF strips and sub-cut as follows:
• Cut five strips into seven 18in lengths and four 8in lengths.
• Sew the remaining nine x WOF strips end to end and cut into four 54in and two 70in lengths.

8 Cut the binding fabric into seven 2½in x WOF strips.

9 Cut the fusible web into five 15in x 18in strips and three 4in strips.

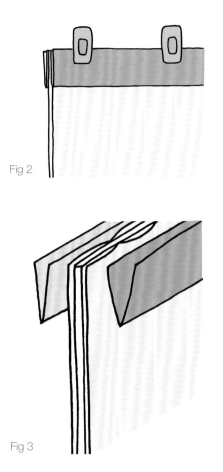

Fig 2

Fig 3

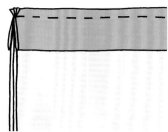

Fig 4

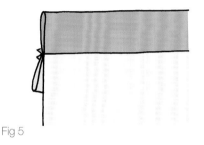

Fig 5

QUILTING THE CENTER STRIPS

10 Baste through all layers of the eighteen QAYG sections to assemble the quilt as follows.

- Eight squares using eight 18in background fabric squares, eight 22in batting squares and eight 22in backing fabric squares.
- Two rectangles using two 9in x 18in background fabric rectangles, two 13in x 22in batting rectangles and two 13 x 22in backing fabric rectangles.
- Four border strips using four 8in x 54in background fabric strips, two 11in x 58in batting strips and two 11in x 58in backing fabric strips.
- Four corner squares using four 8in background fabric squares, two 11in batting squares and two 11in backing fabric squares.

11 Quilt as desired using pale thread. On all but the corner squares, I quilted lines 1in apart—vertical on some blocks

and horizontal on some blocks. On the corner squares, I quilted a diagonal crosshatch pattern of lines 1in apart. When quilting is finished, trim excess batting and backing fabric from all pieces.

12 Join the 18in squares and the 9in x 18in rectangles into three vertical strips as shown in Fig 1. Start by pressing the joining strips in half, wrong sides together, along their length.

13 Clip one 18in front joining strip to the front of one of the blocks with the raw edges aligned. Clip one 18in back joining strip to the back of this same block along the same edge with the raw edges aligned—see Fig 2.

You will be sewing through two layers of the front joining strip, the quilted block and two layers of back joining strip. Fig 3 shows a side view of this. Sew a ¼in seam, joining all three pieces together (Fig 4). Fold up the bottom piece of joining fabric and press well (Fig 5).

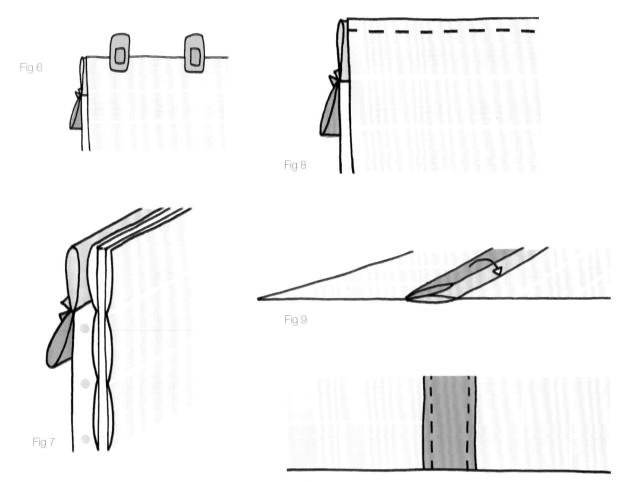

Fig 6

Fig 8

Fig 7

Fig 9

Fig 10

14 Turn over the QAYG section, fold the back joining strip down and fold the front joining strip up. Align and clip the folded edge of the back joining strip to the raw edge of the next quilted block to be joined. The backing fabric on the back of this block should face the back joining strip—see Fig 6. Fig 7 shows a side view of this.

15 Sew a ¼in seam joining these two together (Fig 8). Lay the blocks flat and face up, then press the back joining strip so it lies flat. Fold over and press the top joining strip so that it just overlaps and covers the seam joining the next block to the back joining strip (Fig 9), and topstitch. Topstitch along the second side of this strip so that both sides feature the same topstitching (Fig 10).

16 All the joins will be made using this same method as you continue to piece the quilt, but for now, you are just making the three vertical strips that create the center of the quilt (shown in Fig 1 on page 70).

CREATING THE SCRAPPY TREES

17 Create the scrappy trees as follows: On the five 15in x 18in pieces of fusible web, draw around any large circular dish, bowl or plate—mine was 15in diameter. Draw a randomly placed circle within that first circle by drawing around a smaller plate (e.g. roughly 10in) and finally draw another randomly placed circle within that second circle by drawing around an even smaller plate or bowl (e.g. roughly 5in). The exact sizes, or even the shapes of these dishes, are not important—an oval dish would also create an interestingly shaped tree. See Fig 11 for the kind of tree drawing you are aiming for. Note: Remember that the image will be reversed when you lay it out on the quilt.

18 Randomly draw lines creating 10–12 segments around each of the outer and middle circles. Number each segment in your drawing. It is worth taking a photo of the circles as you draw them so that you can keep track of their placement.

Fig 11

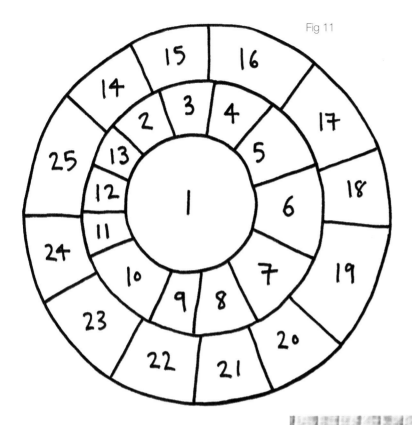

KEY FOR DIAGRAMS

Front joining strips

Back joining strips

Background fabric on front of quilt

Backing fabric on back of quilt

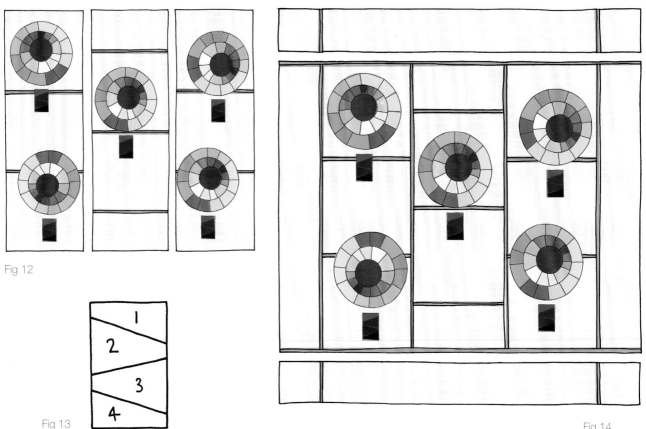

Fig 12

Fig 13

Fig 14

19 Cut along all the lines so that you have a pile of numbered shapes. Fuse each shape to the back of a different colored scrap of fabric. Cut out each shape just very slightly (1/16in or 1/8in) inside the drawn lines, so that the shape you cut out is very slightly smaller than the original drawn shape.

20 Remove the backing paper from the shapes one by one (so you do not lose track of placement), and lay them out on the quilt top. Once they are all positioned, press them in place on the quilt. For a rough layout of the trees on these strips, see Fig 12.

21 Topstitch around the edge of each one (or you could use a zigzag or blanket stitch for a more secure finish). Make five trees in total.

22 The same process is repeated to create the tree trunk. For each tree trunk, cut a piece of fusible web 4in x 8in. Randomly draw three lines on the trunk and number them (Fig 13). Cut out the shapes and fuse to the backs of the fabric scraps, as you did with the tree, and finish in the same way as the tree.

ASSEMBLING THE QUILT

23 The three center strips are joined and the borders added using the same joining method as before. First join the three center strips together, then add two 8in x 54in strips to either side. Add two 8in squares to each end of the two remaining 8in x 54in strips and then add these two border units to the top and bottom of the quilt (Fig 14). The quilt is completely assembled at this stage.

FINISHING

24 Sew the binding strips end to end using diagonal or straight seams, as preferred. Press wrong sides together all along the length to make a double-fold binding. Bind the quilt to finish, taking care to miter the corners neatly (see Techniques: Making Binding Strips and Binding, pages 19 and 20).

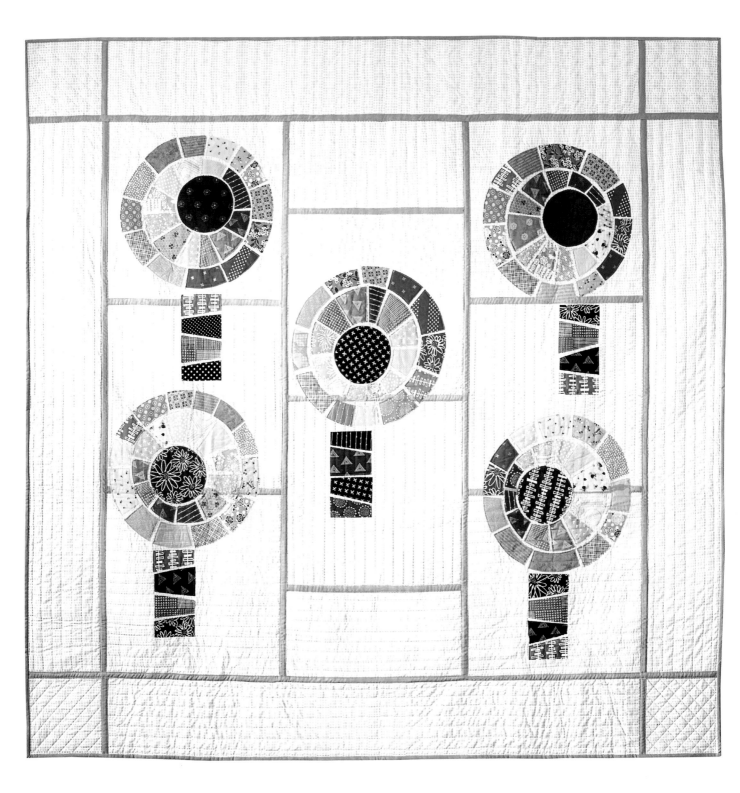

Day for Night Quilt

Brick quilts are very quick and easy to put together, especially in this version where bricks are sewn together into groups then cut apart for speedier piecing. This quilt is a modern version of a traditional Welsh quilt that I saw in a book of old quilts. The first version I made many years ago featured lots of different colors. This color scheme gives the quilt a much simpler feel.

Finished size
64in (163cm) square approx.

Notes
LOF = length of fabric
WOF = width of fabric
QST = quarter-square triangle
Use ¼in seams, unless instructed
    otherwise

Fabrics used
Quilt top and binding: Jardin De
    Provence by Daphne B, licensed by
    Wild Apple for Windham Fabrics
Quilt back: Picture Window in grey
    and red by Suzuko Koseki for Yuwa
    of Japan

You will need
* Four black print fabrics: ½yd (0.5m) of each
* Four beige print fabrics: ½yd (0.5m) of each
* Four cream print fabrics: ¼yd (0.25m) of each
* Backing fabric: 4yds (3.75m)
* Batting: 72in (183cm) square
* Binding fabric: ½yd (0.5m)
* Coordinating piecing and quilting threads

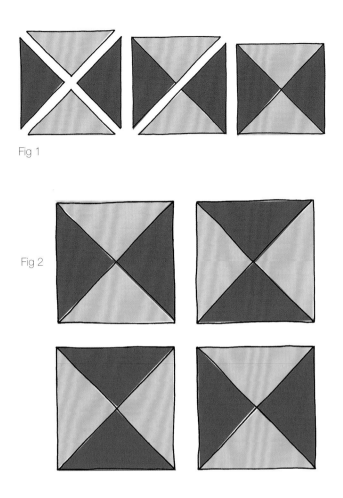

Fig 1

Fig 2

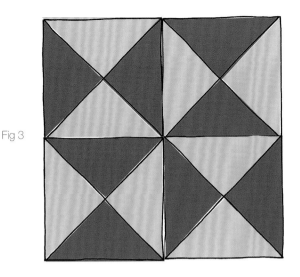

Fig 3

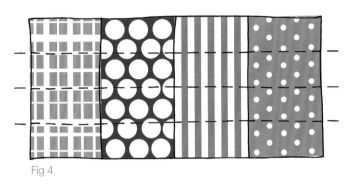

Fig 4

CUTTING

1 Note: The cutting instructions refer to *length* of fabric cuts (LOF) rather than the usual width of fabric cuts. The length of fabric cuts should be made parallel to the selvages (not selvage to selvage). From each of the four black fabrics, cut four 8½in and one 7in x LOF strip. Cut each 7in strip into a 7in square and cut in half along one diagonal to yield two triangles (eight total). Leave the four 8½in x LOF strips whole.

2 Repeat this cutting for the four beige fabrics.

3 From each of the cream fabrics cut five 8½in x LOF strips.

4 Cut the binding fabric into seven 2½in x WOF strips.

5 Cut the backing fabric into two equal lengths.

MAKING THE QUARTER-SQUARE TRIANGLE BLOCKS

6 Sew one black triangle to one beige triangle, and repeat. Sew these two pairs together to make a quarter-square

triangle (QST) unit (Fig 1). Trim the unit to 8½in square, taking care that the seams sit in the corners of the block.

7 Repeat to make the remaining three QST units (Fig 2).

8 Sew these into two rows of two QST units, and then sew these rows together to make the central block, taking care that a beige fabric always sits next to a black fabric (Fig 3). Check that the unit is 16½in square.

ADDING THE BRICK BLOCKS

9 Sew a group of four different black 8½in LOF strips together along the long (LOF) sides (Fig 4). Repeat for the remaining three groups of four different black fabrics.

10 Cut each strip-pieced unit into four 4½in strips, cutting across the seams (Fig 4).

11 Repeat this process with the four beige 8½in strips. Repeat this process with the cream 8½in strips although, since the cream strips are half the length of the black strips, you will only be able to cut two 4½in strips from each piece.

12 You will now add six rounds of bricks around the QST

Fig 5

Fig 6

center unit—two cream, two beige and two black (see the quilt layout in Fig 5). Take care as you add rounds that no two identical fabrics sit next to each other. Begin by ripping out the middle seam in one of the lengths of cream "bricks" to yield two lengths of two. Sew these units to the sides of the central block. Now rip out the end seam in two of the strips of four cream bricks, removing one brick from each strip to yield two strips of three bricks. Sew these to the other two sides of the quilt.

13 Continue this process to add the following rows of bricks, sometimes ripping out seams and sometimes joining shorter strips into longer strips; refer to Fig 5.

- Three cream.
- Four cream.
- Four beige.
- Five beige.
- Five beige.
- Six beige.
- Six black.
- Seven black.
- Seven black.
- Eight black.

QUILTING AND FINISHING

14 Sew the two pieces of backing fabric together along the long sides using a ½in seam and press the seam open. Make a quilt sandwich of the quilt back (right side down), the batting and the quilt top (right side up) (see Techniques: Making a Quilt Sandwich, page 18).

15 Quilt as desired. The quilt shown has a crosshatch pattern of wavy lines 2in apart, using cream thread.

16 When all quilting is finished, square up the quilt, trimming the batting and backing (see Techniques: Squaring Up, page 19).

17 Sew the binding strips end to end using diagonal or straight seams, as preferred. Press wrong sides together all along the length to make a double-fold binding. Bind the quilt to finish, taking care to miter the corners neatly (see Techniques: Making Binding Strips and Binding, pages 19 and 20).

Modern Stars Quilt

This quilt takes the popular morning star block and opens it out into a bigger block by using sashing in between the block units. You can speed up the process by using half-square triangle units, paper pieced in batches for a quicker finish. I used two slightly different background colors (parchment and cream) to create a subtle checkerboard pattern in the quilt. There are so many fantastic solid and semi-solid fabrics currently available that would be perfect for this design.

Finished size
76in (193cm) square approx.

Notes
F8th = fat eighth (9in x 22in approx.)
WOF = width of fabric
HST = half-square triangle
Use ¼in seams, unless instructed otherwise

Fabrics used
Quilt top and binding: Cotton + Steel Basics, Kona parchment (background fabric A), Makower cream Scandi (background fabric B)
Quilt back: Make It Work by Michael Miller Fabrics

You will need
- Twenty-five different print fabrics: a F8th of each
- Background fabric A: 2¾yds (2.5m)
- Background fabric B: 2yds (1.75m)
- Backing fabric: 4¾yds (4.5m)
- Batting: 84in (213cm) square
- Binding fabric: ⅝yd (0.6m)
- Twenty-five foundation paper piecing templates (see page 85)
- Coordinating piecing and quilting threads

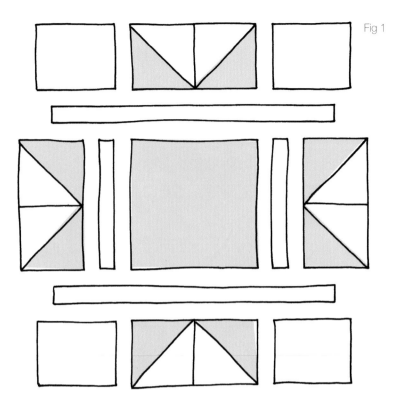

Fig 1

CUTTING

1 Cut each of the twenty-five F8ths into one 6½in square for the block center and one 8½in square for the star points HST.

2 Cut background fabric A as follows:
- Three 8½in x WOF strips. Sub-cut into thirteen 8½in squares (five per strip).
- Thirteen 1½in x WOF strips. Sub-cut each strip into two 1½in x 6½in strips and two 1½in x 14½in strips, to yield twenty-six of each in total.
- Thirteen 3½in x WOF strips. Sub-cut six of those into fifty-two 3½in x 4½in rectangles (nine per strip). Sew the remaining seven strips end to end with straight seams and cut into two 70½in lengths and two 76½in lengths for the borders.

3 Cut background fabric B as follows:
- Three 8½in x WOF strips. Sub-cut into twelve 8½in squares (five per strip).
- Twelve 1½in x WOF strips. Sub-cut each of those into two 1½in x 6½in and two 1½in x 14½in strips, to yield twenty-four of each in total.
- Six 3½in x WOF strips. Sub-cut into forty-eight 3½in x 4½in rectangles (nine per strip).

4 Cut the backing fabric into two equal lengths.

5 Cut the binding fabric into eight 2½in x WOF strips.

MAKING THE HALF-SQUARE TRIANGLE BLOCKS

6 Before starting to make the blocks, decide on the layout of the twenty-five fabrics. Thirteen of the print fabrics will be paired with the A background fabric and twelve will be paired with B background fabric. The A and B background fabrics form a subtle checkerboard pattern. The quilt assembly is shown in Fig 2, so refer to that for guidance (background fabric A is used in the four blocks in each corner of the quilt and the outer border).

7 Start by making the HST units, as follows: Pin one background 8½in square and one print 8½in square to the back of each of the twenty-five paper templates, with the fabrics right sides together and the background fabric next to the paper. Shorten your machine stitch length to 14 to 18 stitches per inch and sew along all of the blue lines.

8 Cut the template and fabric along all the green lines using a rotary cutter. Trim off the corners on each triangle along the red lines.

9 Press each HST unit open. Remove the paper from the back of each unit. Each unit should be 3½in square.

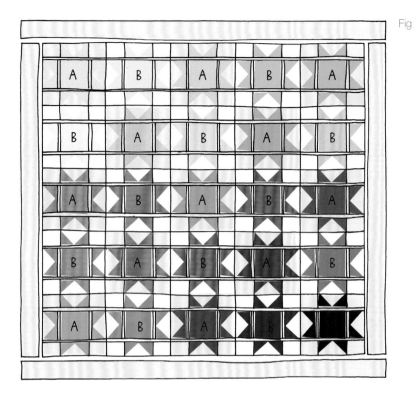

Fig 2

ASSEMBLING THE BLOCKS

10 Assemble each block as follows (see Fig 1). Take care to use the correct A or B background fabric pieces when adding strips and rectangles to HST units. Start by sewing the HSTs into four pairs, with the background fabric together.

11 Sew 3½in x 4½in rectangles to each end of two of those units. Sew 1½in x 6½in strips of background fabric to each side of the central 6½in square.

12 Sew the two remaining HST units to either side of this central unit.

13 Sew the five rows of the block together using 1½in x 14½in strips of background fabric between the top and the center row and between the bottom and the center row.

14 Repeat this process to make the remaining twenty-four blocks.

ASSEMBLING THE QUILT

15 Arrange your twenty-five blocks into five rows each with five blocks (see Fig 2). Sew the blocks together into rows, pressing the seams in opposite directions in each row. Sew the five rows together, matching seams carefully.

16 Pin and sew the 3½in x 70½in borders to the sides of the quilt. Press seams outwards. Add the 3½in x 76½in strips to the top and bottom of the quilt and press seams outwards.

QUILTING AND FINISHING

17 Sew the two pieces of backing fabric together along the long sides using a ½in seam and press the seam open. Make a quilt sandwich of the quilt back (right side down), the batting and the quilt top (right side up) (see Techniques: Making a Quilt Sandwich, page 18).

18 Quilt as desired. The quilt shown has a diagonal cross-hatch pattern of lines about 2in apart, using cream thread.

19 When all the quilting is finished, square up the quilt, trimming the batting and backing (see Techniques: Squaring Up, page 19).

20 Sew the binding strips together end to end using diagonal seams or straight seams, as preferred. Press wrong sides together all along the length to make a double-fold binding. Bind the quilt to finish, taking care to miter the corners neatly (see Techniques: Making Binding Strips and Binding, pages 19 and 20).

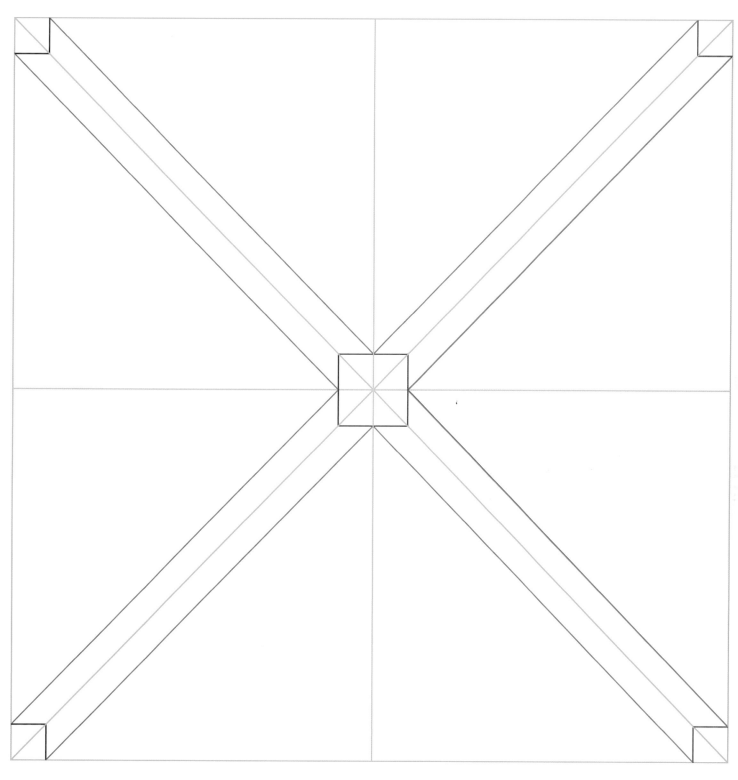

MODERN STARS
Foundation paper piecing template for half-square triangles
Full size (100%)

Festive Stars Quilt

I love making quilts with simple, outsized blocks. This one is made with just nine blocks that come together quite quickly because they are paper pieced, so no time is wasted cutting templates. Although Christmas-themed fabrics are used in this quilt, they could easily be replaced with summer fabrics for a bright picnic blanket, or any colors to match the décor in your home.

Finished size
67in (170cm) square approx.

Notes
F8th = fat eighth (9in x 22in approx.)
WOF = width of fabric
Use ¼in seams, unless instructed
    otherwise

Fabrics used
Quilt top, back and binding: A Merry
    Little Christmas by Riley Blake,
    plus a black and white dot for
    the background

You will need
- Black dot background fabric: 3½yds (3.25m)
- Variety of fabrics for stars: eighteen F8ths
- White dot cornerstone fabric: ¼yd (0.25m)
- Backing fabric: 4¼yds (4m)
- Batting: 75in (190cm) square
- Binding fabric: ½yd (0.5m)
- Thirty-six A and thirty-six B templates (see pages 90–91)
- Coordinating piecing and quilting threads

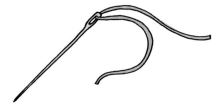

Fig 1

CUTTING

1 From the black dot background fabric, cut nineteen 3½in x WOF strips. Sub-cut these strips as follows:
- Cut six strips into twelve 3½in squares each and cut those in half along one diagonal to yield a total of 144 triangles. These will be used for sections 2 and 3 on template A and sections 4 and 5 on template B.
- Cut five strips into seven 5½in pieces each (to yield thirty-five). These will be used for section 4 on template A.
- Cut seven strips into five 8½in pieces (to yield thirty-five). These will be used for section 5 on template A.
- Cut the final strip into one 5½in piece and one 8½in piece. These will be used for sections 4 and 5 on template A (so you have thirty-six pieces for each section in total).

2 From the black dot background fabric, cut five 4½in x WOF strips. Sub-cut these strips as follows:
- Cut four strips into nine 4½in squares and cut those in half along one diagonal to yield a total of seventy-two triangles. These will be used to piece sections 2 and 3 on template B.
- Cut the remaining strip into nine 4½in squares. These will be used to piece the center of each block.

3 From the black dot background fabric, cut twelve 3in x WOF strips. Sub-cut these strips into two 19½in lengths each, to yield a total of twenty-four sashing strips.

4 Cut each star F8th (two per star) into four 8in x 5in

rectangles. These will be used to foundation paper piece section 1 on each template.

5 From the white dot cornerstone fabric, cut two 3in x WOF strips. Sub-cut these strips into sixteen 3in squares.

6 Cut the backing fabric into two equal lengths and remove selvages.

7 Cut the binding fabric into seven 2½in x WOF strips.

PIECING THE BLOCKS

8 Using the templates on pages 90–91, foundation paper piece four template A and four template B for each block with two coordinating star fabrics and the black dot background; use the fabric pieces that have been pre-cut to speed up the process. Reduce your machine stitch length to 14 to 18 stitches per inch and piece the templates in the number order shown on the templates. Refer to Techniques: Foundation Paper Piecing, page 16, for full instructions and diagrams on this technique.

9 Trim each unit to size along the outer dashed line—unit A should be 8in square and unit B should be 8in x 4½in. Remove the backing papers.

10 Lay out the units for each block—four pieced A units, four pieced B units and one 4½in background fabric square, as shown in Fig 1. Sew the units into three rows, nesting the

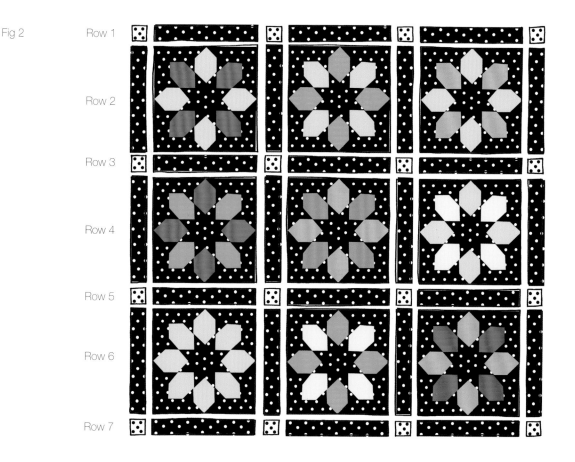

Fig 2
Row 1
Row 2
Row 3
Row 4
Row 5
Row 6
Row 7

seams. Press seams away from the center in the top and bottom rows and towards the center in the middle row.

11 Sew the three rows together to make the finished block. The block should measure 19½in square. Make nine blocks in total.

ASSEMBLING THE QUILT

12 Sew the blocks, cornerstones and sashing strips into seven rows as follows, pressing seams towards the sashing strips throughout (see the quilt layout in Fig 2):
• For rows 1, 3, 5 and 7, sew together four cornerstones and three sashing strips.
• For rows 2, 4 and 6, sew together four sashing strips and three blocks.

13 Sew all seven rows together, nesting seams and pressing seams to one side or open, as preferred.

QUILTING AND FINISHING

14 Sew the two pieces of backing fabric together along the long sides using a ½in seam and press the seam open. Make a quilt sandwich of the quilt back (right side down), the batting and the quilt top (right side up) (see Techniques: Making a Quilt Sandwich, page 18).

15 Quilt as desired. The quilt shown was quilted with a diagonal crosshatch pattern of lines 1½in apart, using white thread.

16 When all the quilting is finished, square up the quilt, trimming the batting and backing (see Techniques: Squaring Up, page 19).

17 Sew the binding strips together end to end using diagonal seams, or straight seams if preferred. Press wrong sides together all along the length to make a double-fold binding. Bind the quilt to finish, taking care to miter the corners neatly (see Techniques: Making Binding Strips and Binding, pages 19 and 20).

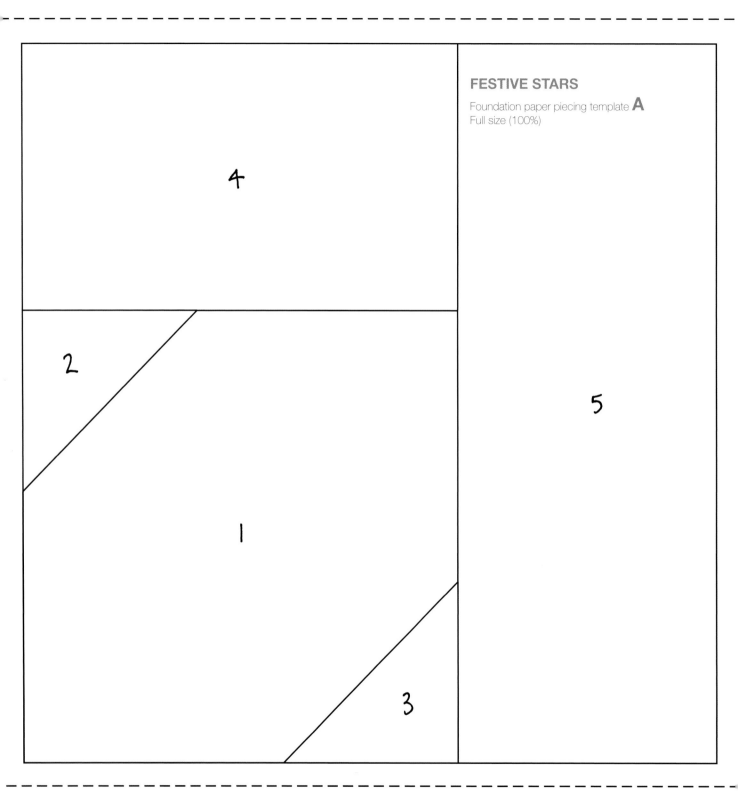

FESTIVE STARS

Foundation paper piecing template **A**
Full size (100%)

4

2

1

3

5

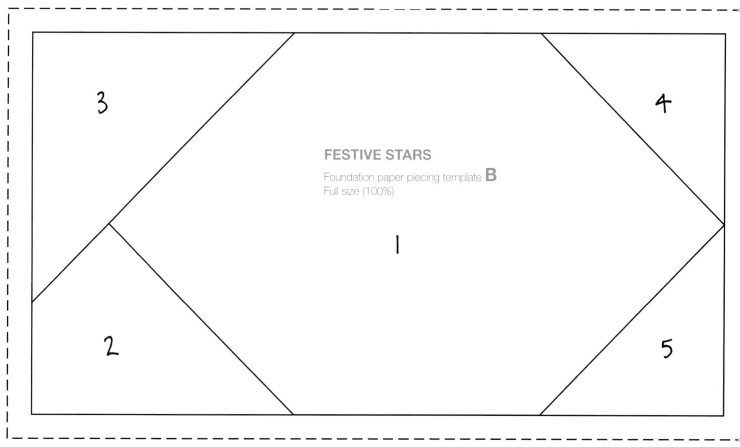

FESTIVE STARS

Foundation paper piecing template **B**
Full size (100%)

3

4

1

2

5

Stormy Sea Wall Hanging

The design for this quilt came from a bundle of fabrics, where the colors and shapes in the prints have the feel of a dark English sea on a stormy day with grey clouds in the sky—very different to a bright aqua Mediterranean Sea on a hot, still day. I divided the sections into three, imagining the view from inside a house overlooking the sea. The sections were then pieced using a very organic approach, randomly cutting wavy strips—just the opposite of the usual precise, geometric shapes in traditional quilts. This gives the image those fluid, unpredictable shapes you see rippling across the sea and sky on a stormy day.

Finished size
19in x 35½in (48cm x 90cm) approx.

Notes
F8th = fat eighth (9in x 22in approx.)
FQ = fat quarter
WOF = width of fabric
Use ¼in seams, unless instructed
  otherwise

Fabrics used
Quilt top and binding: Nocturne by
  Janet Clare for Moda Fabrics
Quilt back: Robert Kaufman Kona Putty

You will need
- Cream fabric for "frame": one F8th
- Sea-colored fabrics: twelve to fourteen scrap pieces equivalent to about four FQs in total and each 22in wide minimum
- Backing fabric: ¾yd (0.75m)
- Batting: 23in x 40in (60cm x 100cm)
- Binding fabric: ¼yd (0.25m)
- Spray starch
- Coordinating piecing and quilting threads

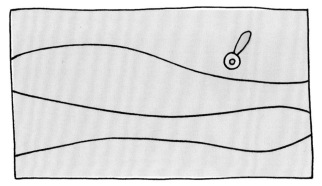

Fig 1
Cut three random wavy lines across the width and use the two center strips.

CUTTING OUT

1 You need approximately twelve to fourteen scraps of sea-colored fabric ranging from dark to light. You will need to cut two strips from each piece. (For more variety, you can use more fabrics but just cut one strip from some of them.) You may need to use more than fourteen fabrics or fewer than twelve for each section of the quilt depending on how wide you cut them. Each piece you cut must be the width of a fat quarter (22in).

2 Press each piece of fabric and then lay each one in turn on your cutting mat. Cut three random wavy lines across the width of each piece, roughly between 1in and 3in wide. This will give you two random strips with curved edges — the top and bottom pieces can be discarded (see Fig 1).

3 Cut the cream sashing fabric for the "frame" into five 1in x 22in strips. Sub-cut these strips into four 18in lengths and one 19½in length.

4 Cut the backing fabric to 23in x 40in (60cm x 100cm).

5 Cut the binding fabric into three 2½in x WOF strips. Cut one of these strips into two 20in lengths and the other two strips to 35½in long.

JOINING THE STRIPS

6 Divide the fabric strips into two piles with one strip of each fabric in each. Lay out the two sets of strips in order from dark to light. Take the darkest two and sew them together. When sewing these curves, you will need to adjust both fabric pieces constantly as you run them through the machine, so that the edges of both are always aligning with the ¼in position on your sewing machine or machine foot. If you have not tried this technique before, you should practice first on scraps.

7 Press the seam open after one has been sewn — this will help the bumpy seam to lay flat. Once the seam is pressed open, select full steam on your iron and iron the seam flat, using the steam, the weight of the iron and a back-and-forth ironing movement (as opposed to pressing) to press the fabrics flat. Join the next strip in the same way, pressing after each seam and then ironing flat using the steam to help you. Don't worry about what the side edges of the fabric look like as these will be trimmed later.

8 Once all strips are joined together and ironed flat, measure the piece you have made and check that it is a *minimum* of 19½in wide by 18in tall. If it is not yet tall enough, add an extra strip at the top, bottom or both until it reaches 18in.

9 Use spray starch to make the assembled piece lie flat, as follows: Lay the piece on a flat surface that is covered by an old towel. Press the piece as flat as possible and then spray it liberally with starch. Press the whole piece again until it lies perfectly flat. Allow it to dry for a few minutes; it will become quite stiff.

10 Place the whole piece on your cutting mat and trim to 18in tall. Now cut three vertical strips each 6½in wide from this piece; set aside.

11 Repeat this process for the second set of strips.

ADDING THE SASHING

12 Take the three top pieces and join them together using two of the 1in x 18in strips of sashing fabric, taking care to put the pieced units in the same order as they were cut, so that the pattern continues from one frame to the next to the next. This assembly is shown in Fig 2. Press seams towards the sashing. Repeat this for the bottom three pieces.

13 Now add the 1in x 19½in sashing strip to join the top and bottom of the quilt. Press towards the sashing to finish.

QUILTING AND FINISHING

14 Make a quilt sandwich of the quilt back (right side down), the batting and the quilt top (right side up) (see Techniques: Making a Quilt Sandwich, page 18).

15 Quilt as desired. The quilt shown was quilted with wavy horizontal lines very close together following the lines of the seams, using navy, blue, grey and cream threads.

16 When all quilting is finished, square up the quilt, trimming the batting and backing (see Techniques: Squaring Up, page 19).

Fig 2

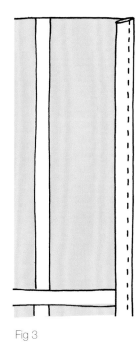

Fig 3

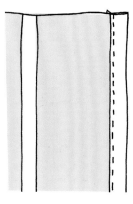

Fig 4

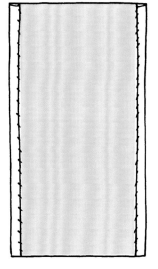

Fig 5

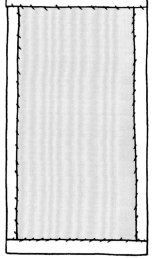

Fig 6

17 Press the two shorter and two longer binding strips in half along the length wrong sides together. Sew the two longer strips to each of the longer sides of the quilt, raw edges aligned, right sides together (Fig 3). Press the binding strips flat and topstitch along the edge, approximately 1/8in away from the folded edge (Fig 4). Fold the binding completely around the back of the quilt so it cannot be seen from the front; press and hand-stitch in place as you would stitch a quilt binding (Fig 5).

18 Repeat the process using the shorter strips on the top and bottom. When attached they should overhang each end by about 1/2in. This overhang can be tucked under once the strips are being hand-sewn to the back (Fig 6).

Rainbow Leaves Runner

This attractive runner is created using fusible web to make the orange peel or leaf shapes. A white background gives a lovely fresh and contemporary look to the design. The shapes are quick and easy to cut using a dinner plate as a guide and a rotary cutter. You'll avoid tracing templates and careful scissor cutting, which can take much longer.

Finished size
25in x 89in (63.5cm x 226cm) approx.

Notes
WOF = width of fabric
Use ¼in seams, unless instructed
  otherwise

Fabrics used
Quilt top and binding: Two 5in square
  packs of Blueberry Park by Karen
  Lewis for Robert Kaufman, plus
  Robert Kaufman Kona White
Quilt back: Quilt Back by Whistler
  Studios for Windham Fabrics

You will need
- Colored print fabrics for leaves: fifty-seven 5in squares
  of different fabrics
- White fabric: 2¼yds (2m)
- Backing fabric: 2¾yds (2.5m)
- Batting: 33in x 97in (85cm x 245cm)
- Binding fabric: ½yd (0.5m)
- Fusible web: 2¾yds (2.5m) of 18in (46cm) wide
- Dinner plate: approx. 10in (25.5cm) diameter
- Zigzag blade for rotary cutter (optional)
- Coordinating piecing and quilting threads

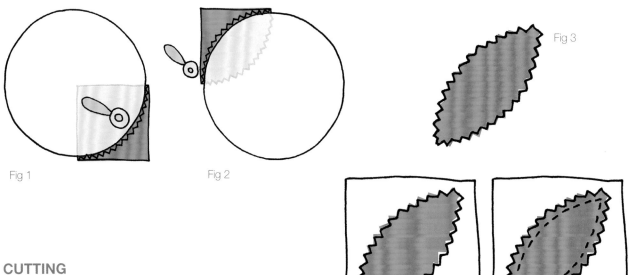

Fig 1

Fig 2

Fig 3

Fig 4

Fig 5

CUTTING

1 From the white fabric, cut eight 5½in x WOF strips. Sub-cut these strips into seven 5½in squares each, to yield a total of fifty-six (you need fifty-seven but one more square is cut in the next step).

2 From the white fabric, cut three 6in x WOF strips. From two of these strips cut seven 6in squares. From the third strip cut one 6in square and one 5½in square. Cut the fifteen 6in squares in half along one diagonal to yield thirty triangles in total.

3 From the white fabric, cut six 2½in x WOF strips. Cut one of the 2½in strips into two 21½in lengths for the border. Sew the remaining five strips end to end with straight seams and cut into two 89½in lengths for the border. Note: You may prefer to wait until the runner is pieced before you cut these border strips.

4 Cut the fusible web into nineteen 5in strips. Sub-cut each of these strips into three 5in squares, to yield fifty-seven in total.

5 Cut the binding fabric into six 2½in x WOF strips.

CREATING THE LEAVES

6 Fuse each 5in square of fusible web onto the back of each colored 5in square. Remove the paper.

7 Using the zigzag blade (or a regular one) in the rotary cutter, cut one leaf from each square using the dinner plate as a guide (see Figs 1, 2 and 3). Cut one from each of the fifty-seven 5in squares.

8 Fuse each leaf to one white 5½in square, as shown in Fig 4. Sew a line of straight stitching approximately ⅛in from the edge of each leaf to secure (Fig 5).

ASSEMBLING THE RUNNER

9 Lay out the squares and triangles into fifteen rows as follows (see Fig 6):
- Rows 1 and 15—two triangles.
- Rows 2 and 14—two triangles and two leaves.
- Rows 3 and 13—two triangles and four leaves.
- Rows 4 to 12—two triangles and five leaves.

10 Sew the leaves and triangles into the fifteen rows. Press seams in opposite directions in each row.

11 Sew the fifteen rows together, taking care to nest seams. Press seams open or to one side, as preferred. Carefully trim the sides to ¼in beyond the corners of the leaf squares, if necessary.

ADDING THE BORDER

12 Measure your runner across the center width—it should be 21½in; if not, make a note of the measurement of *your* runner. Take the white 2½in wide border strips and cut two strips to your measurement (or 21½in). Sew these strips to the shorter sides of the runner, pinning in place at the center first, and then the sides and then in between, to make sure the strips fit the runner correctly. Press seams away from the center.

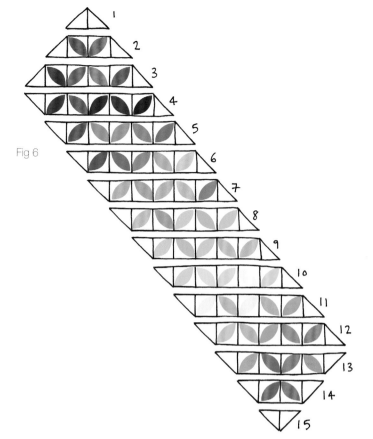

Fig 6

13 Measure your runner across the center length—it should be 89½in; if not, make a note of the measurement of *your* runner. Using the white 2½in wide border strips, cut two strips to your measurement (or 89½in). Sew these strips to the longer sides of the runner, pinning as before. Press seams outwards.

QUILTING AND FINISHING

14 Make a quilt sandwich of the quilt back (right side down), the batting and the quilt top (right side up) (see Techniques: Making a Quilt Sandwich, page 18).

15 Quilt as desired. The runner shown was quilted with lines ½in apart going across the runner, using pale thread.

16 When all quilting is finished, square up the runner, trimming the batting and backing (see Techniques: Squaring Up, page 19).

17 Sew the binding strips together end to end using diagonal seams or straight seams, as preferred. Press wrong sides together all along the length to make a double-fold binding. Bind the runner to finish, taking care to miter the corners neatly (see Techniques: Making Binding Strips and Binding, pages 19 and 20).

The Planets Mini Quilt

This would make a perfect quilt for any child who loves the night sky – I called it The Planets because it reminded me of the charts showing the planets lined up in different sizes. If you have a die cutter, the quilt goes together even more quickly because you can use it to cut out the circles. If not, you can still cut the circles out— you just need to take a little more time. Using fusible web appliqué means this quilt is a quick one to assemble.

Finished size
36in x 40in (90cm x 102cm) approx.

Notes
WOF = width of fabric
F8th = fat eighth (9in x 22in approx.)
Use ¼in seams, unless instructed
   otherwise

Fabrics used
Quilt top: Mon Ami by BasicGrey for
   Moda Fabrics and cream Linea by
   Makower UK
Quilt back: Quilt Back by Whistler
   Studios for Windham Fabrics
Binding: Mon Ami by BasicGrey for
   Moda Fabrics

You will need
- Background fabric: 1¼yds (1.25m)
- Dark grey fabrics: four F8ths in total
- Light grey fabrics: two F8ths in total (I used more prints
   for variety)
- Light blue fabrics: two F8ths in total (I used more prints
   for variety)
- Red fabrics: three F8ths in total
- Backing fabric: 1³⁄₈yds (1.25m)
- Batting: 44in x 48in (112cm x 122cm)
- Binding fabric: ³⁄₈yd (0.3m)
- Fusible web: 2yds (2m) of 18in (46cm) wide
- One set of circle templates (see page 103)
- Coordinating piecing and quilting threads

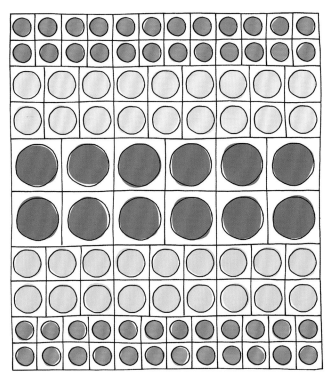

Fig 1

CUTTING

1 Cut the background fabric into two 6½in x WOF strips, four 4½in x WOF strips and four 3½in x WOF strips. Cut these strips into twelve 6½in squares, thirty-six 4½in squares and forty-eight 3½in squares.

2 Cut the binding fabric into four 2½in x WOF strips.

MAKING THE CIRCLE APPLIQUÉS

3 Trace twelve 5in circle templates, thirty-six 3in circle templates and forty-eight 2in circle templates onto the paper side of the fusible web. Cut out the fusible web circles a little outside of the marked lines.

4 Fuse the twelve 5in circles onto the back of the dark grey fabrics, eighteen of the 3in circles onto the back of the light grey fabrics, eighteen of the 3in circles onto the back of the light blue fabrics and the 2in circles onto the back of the red fabrics. Cut out all of the circles neatly on the drawn lines and remove the backing papers.

5 Fuse the circles in place on the background squares as follows:
• Fuse the 5in dark grey circles onto the middle of the 6½in background squares.
• Fuse the 3in light grey and light blue circles onto the middle of the 4½in background squares.
• Fuse the 2in red circles onto the middle of the 3½in background squares.
Once fused, secure the circles in place with a straight, zigzag or blanket stitch around the edges.

ASSEMBLING THE QUILT

6 Sew the appliquéd blocks into ten rows as shown in Fig 1, pressing the seams in opposite directions in each row. Use the following order for the rows:
• Two rows with twelve red circles in each.
• Two rows with nine light grey circles in each.
• Two rows with six dark grey circles in each.
• Two rows with nine light blue circles in each.
• Two rows with twelve red circles in each.

7 Sew the ten rows together to finish the quilt top.

QUILTING AND FINISHING

8 Make a quilt sandwich of the quilt back (right side down), the batting and the quilt top (right side up) (see Techniques: Making a Quilt Sandwich, page 18).

9 Quilt as desired. The quilt shown was quilted in free-motion wavy lines with loops and swirls in them, using pale thread.

10 When all quilting is finished, square up the quilt, trimming the batting and backing (see Techniques: Squaring Up, page 19).

11 Sew the binding strips together end to end using diagonal seams, or straight seams, as preferred. Press wrong sides together all along the length to make a double-fold binding. Bind the quilt to finish, taking care to miter the corners neatly (see Techniques: Making Binding Strips and Binding, pages 19 and 20).

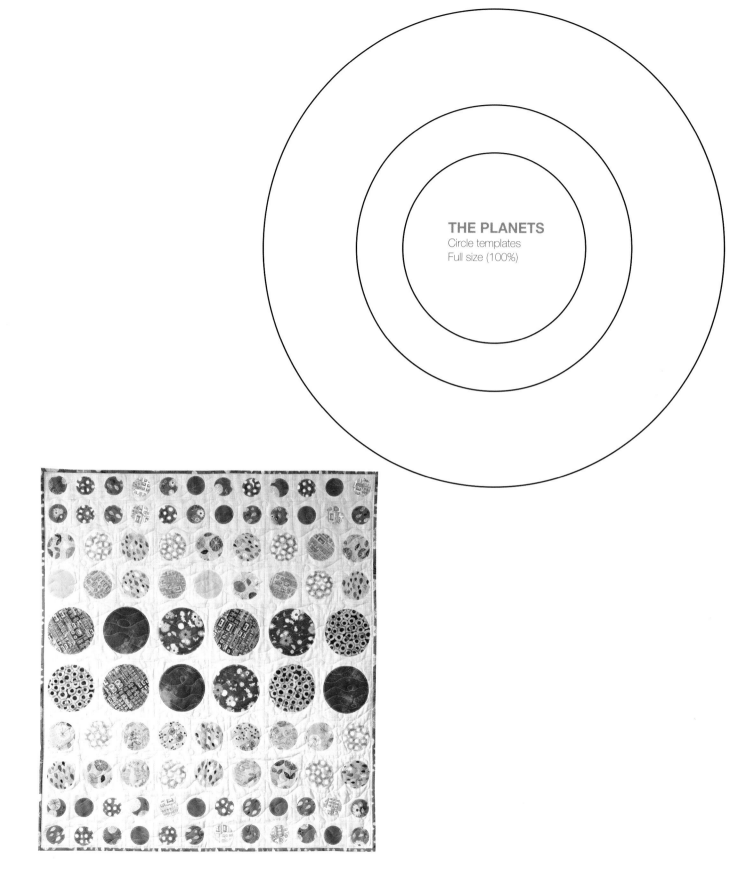

THE PLANETS
Circle templates
Full size (100%)

Gypsy Pillow

The bright fabrics in this project are cut into wedges to make a quick, fun circular pillow. You could add a fabric-covered button into the center as an additional decorative feature or add piping between the sides and the top and bottom, but I've kept it simple for a quick and easy to make project.

Finished size
17in (43cm) diameter approx.

Notes
FQ = fat quarter
Use ¼in seams, unless instructed otherwise

Fabrics used
Pillow top: Glow by Amy Butler for Rowan Fabrics
Pillow back and side: Wovens by Kaffe Fassett for Rowan Fabrics

You will need
- Pillow top fabrics: nine 5in x 10in (13cm x 25.5cm) rectangles from assorted prints
- Pillow side: one FQ
- Pillow back: one FQ
- Batting: one 20in (50cm) square and one piece 6in x 65in (15cm x 165cm)
- Zipper: 15in–17in (35cm–40cm) long
- One wedge template (see page 107)
- Coordinating piecing and quilting threads
- Circular pillow form or dense foam to fit cover, 17in (40cm) diameter x 4in (10cm) deep

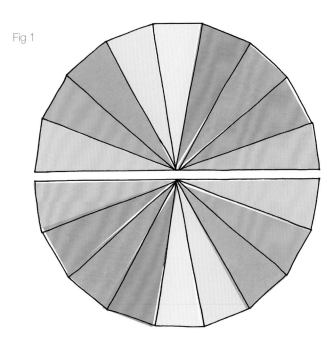

Fig 1

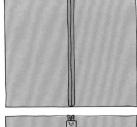

Fig 2
A
With right sides facing, sew back pieces together. Open flat, wrong sides facing up.

B
Center the zipper right side down on back seam and sew ⅛in to either side of teeth. Zigzag-stitch at top and bottom of zipper.

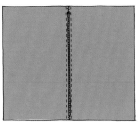

C
On the right side, rip out seam over the zipper teeth between top and bottom zigzag stitching to access zipper.

CUTTING

1 Cut each of the pillow fabrics into two wedges each using the template as a guide for a total of eighteen wedges. For the first wedge, align the long edge of the template with the long edge of the rectangle. For the second wedge, rotate the template 180 degrees.

2 Cut the pillow side fabric into three 5in x 21in strips.

3 Cut the pillow back fabric into two 18in x 11in pieces.

MAKING THE PILLOW

4 Sew the wedges into two identical sets of nine. Now sew the two sets together to make a circle (Fig 1). Press all seams open.

5 Sew the three side fabric pieces together end to end to make one long strip. Press the seams open.

6 Sew the two pillow back pieces together along the 18in side and press the seam open (see Fig 2A). Sew the zipper to the back of this seam, then open the seam just as far as each end of the zipper. Secure the top and bottom of the zipper and the seams by zigzag-stitching by machine or by hand (see Figs 2B and 2C).

QUILTING AND FINISHING

7 Baste the batting pieces to the pillow top and the pillow side piece and quilt as desired. I quilted circular lines around the pillow top and horizontal lines along the pillow side, sewing all lines about ½in apart. Trim the excess batting from each piece and trim the seam ends on the pillow so it is circular (Fig 3). The pillow front should measure 18in across once trimmed.

8 Use the pillow top as a guide to cut the pillow back to a circle of the same size.

9 Using a ¼in seam, sew the pillow side to the pillow top, leaving a couple of inches unsewn at each end. Now join the two ends together (you may have to trim the pillow side to fit). Continue sewing the remainder of the side to the pillow top.

10 Now open the zipper partially and sew the pillow back to the pillow side, again using a ¼in seam.

11 Turn the pillow right side out, insert the pillow form and close the zipper to finish.

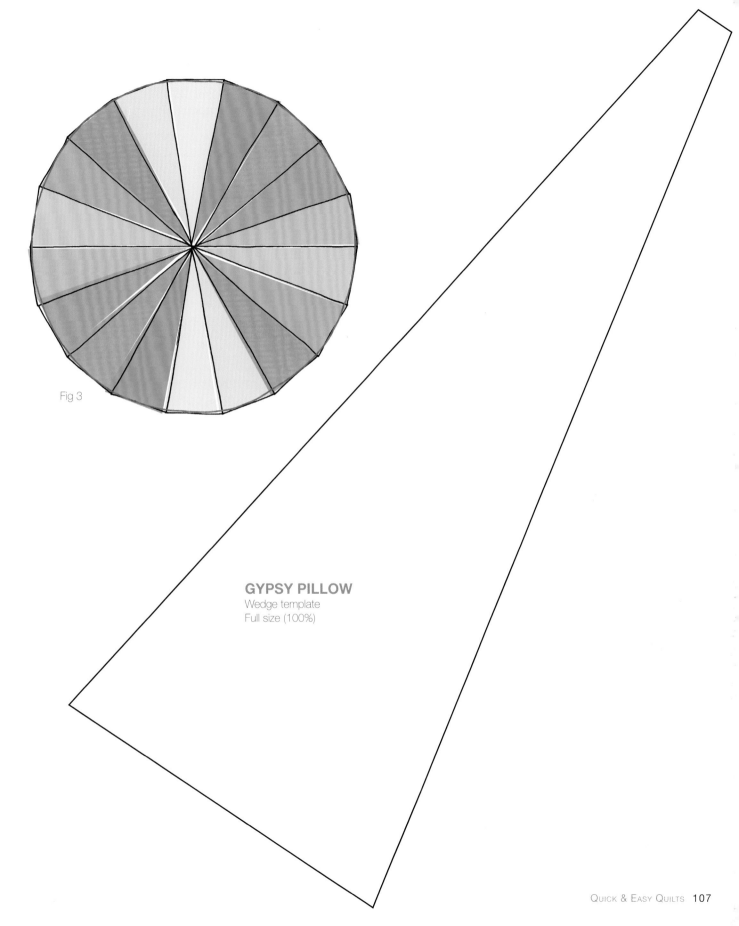

Fig 3

GYPSY PILLOW
Wedge template
Full size (100%)

Three Primary Pillows

Half-square triangle units are used in these three pillows to create a bold design, while the solid fabrics make the traditional block look very modern. The half-square triangles are foundation paper pieced, which makes them very quick to make and very accurate, without any time-consuming trimming! The instructions are the same for each pillow. Each pillow is finished with a wide stitched flange around the outside.

Finished size
23in (58cm) square approx.

Notes
F8th = fat eighth (9in x 22in approx.)
HST = half-square triangle
Use ¼in seams, unless instructed
   otherwise

Fabrics used
Pillow tops: Black, white, red, yellow
   and blue solid fabrics
Pillow backs: Black and white gingham
   from Makower UK

You will need (per pillow)
- Black solid fabric: ½yd (0.5m)
- White solid fabric: ¼yd (0.25m)
- Red, blue or yellow solid fabric: one F8th
- Fabric for pillow back: ¾yd (0.75m)
- Batting: 27in (70cm) square
- Three Modern Stars templates (see page 85) and three Primary Pillows templates (see page 111)
- Coordinating piecing and quilting threads
- Three 18in (46cm) pillow forms

CUTTING (PER PILLOW)

1 From the black solid fabric cut the following pieces:
* Two 9in x 13in rectangles.
* Two 3in x 18½in strips for border.
* Two 3in x 23½in strips for border.

2 From the white solid, cut three 9in x 13in rectangles.

3 Cut one solid 9in x 13in rectangle for each pillow—red, yellow and blue.

4 From the pillow back fabric, cut two pieces for each pillow, one 23½in x 13in and one 23½in x 17in.

MAKING THE HST UNITS

5 For each pillow, copy or photocopy three Modern Stars templates (page 85) and three Primary Pillows templates (page 111). Trim each Primary Pillows template along the heavy green line and tape to one end or side of a Modern Star template to make one larger template.

6 Pin one white 9in x 13in rectangle and one black 9in x 13in rectangle to the back of one of the paper templates, with the fabrics right sides together and the white fabric next to the paper.

7 Shorten your machine stitch to 14 to 18 stitches per inch and sew carefully along all of the blue lines.

8 Cut the template and fabric along all the green lines using a rotary cutter and ruler. Trim off the corners on each triangle along the red lines.

9 Press each HST unit open. Each unit will be 3½in square. Remove the paper from the back of each unit.

10 For each pillow, repeat steps 6 through 9 with the following color combinations:
* Black and white fabric rectangles.
* Red, blue or yellow and white fabric rectangles.
You should have a total of twenty-four black/white HST units and twelve color/white HST units per pillow.

Fig 1

Fig 2

ASSEMBLING THE PILLOW FRONT

11 Arrange the HSTs in six rows of six as shown in Fig 1, taking care to rotate units as necessary to achieve the correct pattern for the block. Sew the units together in rows, pressing seams in opposite directions in each row. Sew the six rows together, nesting seams, and press seams open or to one side, as preferred.

12 Add the border strips to each pillow front, adding the two 3in x 18½in strips to the top and bottom first and pressing seams towards the border strips. Now add the 3in x 23½in strips to the sides and press seams towards the border strips (Fig 2).

QUILTING AND FINISHING

13 Make a quilt sandwich of the pillow front and the batting. If desired, you could also add a piece of backing fabric to this, using a piece of unwanted fabric the same size as the batting so the batting doesn't get caught in the feed dogs.

14 Quilt as desired. On the pillows shown, a diagonal cross-

hatch pattern was marked using a hera marker, with lines 1¼in apart, set ½in on either side of the main diagonal seam lines. Black thread was used for the quilting. When all quilting is finished, trim the pillow square, removing excess batting and backing. Each pillow front should measure 23½in square.

15 On each of the pillow back pieces, turn over a ½in hem, twice, on one long side and press. Sew this hem with matching thread.

16 Place the pillow front right side up. Place the narrower pillow back piece on top, right side down, with the hem at the center and all outer edges aligned. Add the wider pillow back piece right side down, aligning all outer edges. The two back pieces will overlap across the center.

17 Sew the pillow front and the pillow back pieces together all around the edge using a ¼in seam. Clip corners, turn right side out and press the seams flat.

18 Topstitch the front of the pillow to the back, along the line where the black border meets the center section of the pillow, to create the flange effect. Insert the pillow form to finish.

PRIMARY PILLOWS

Foundation paper piecing template for half-square triangles
Full size (100%)

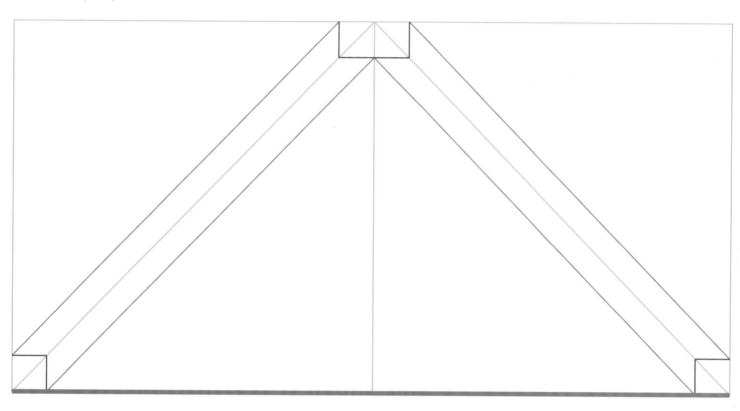

Out on the Ocean Mini Quilt

The blocks in this quilt are quick and fun to make as they need no careful measuring. I used blues and greys to suggest sea and sky but you could use greens to suggest fields or even random colors for a more abstract effect. Since there is no careful measuring and each cut is random, no two pieces made this way would ever be the same.

Finished size
42½in (108cm) square approx.

Notes
WOF = width of fabric
F16th = fat sixteenth (9in x 11in approx.)
Use ¼in seams, unless instructed otherwise

Fabrics used
Quilt top and binding: Blueberry Park by Karen Lewis for Robert Kaufman, Robert Kaufman Kona White, solids from Oakshott shot cottons and Robert Kaufman Kona solids
Quilt back: Oakshott Charcoal

You will need
- Sea fabrics: eighteen F16ths (9in x 11in)
- Sky fabrics: eighteen F16ths (9in x 11in)
- White fabric: 2yds (1.75m)
- Backing fabric: 2¾yds (2.5m)
- Batting: 50in (127cm) square
- Binding fabric: ³⁄₈yd (0.4m)
- Coordinating piecing and quilting threads

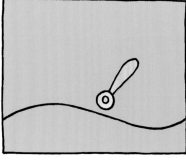

Fig 1

Fig 3

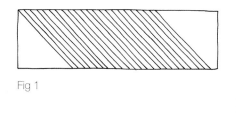

Fig 2

CUTTING

1 Cut the white fabric into six 1in, four 2in and six 9in x WOF strips. Sub-cut these strips as follows:

• Cut the 1in x WOF strips into twelve 10in lengths and three 40in lengths, for the sashing.

• Cut the 2in x WOF strips into two 40in lengths and two 43in lengths, for the border.

• Cut the 9in x WOF strips into twenty-two 1in x 12in bias-cut strips (see Fig 1).

2 Cut the backing fabric into two equal lengths.

3 Cut the binding fabric into five 2½in x WOF strips.

MAKING THE BLOCKS

4 You will be making eight 10in square sea blocks and eight 10in square sky blocks. Each block will use nine different sea fabrics and eight 1in x 12in white bias strips. Each row of four blocks uses one set of nine fabrics pieced in the same order.

5 Take one sea F16th placed landscape style and make a wavy cut approximately a quarter of the way up (Fig 2).

6 With right sides together, sew one 1in x 12in white bias strip to the wavy edge of this piece, pinning and easing in any fullness as you pin and sew. Flip up the bias strip and press seams away from the sea fabric (Fig 3). Each time you add a fabric, press the seam area with a back-and-forth ironing motion, using steam as necessary to get the area to lie flat. If it doesn't lie perfectly flat, don't worry because you can smooth the area when you are quilting the mini quilt.

7 Lay the next sea F16th underneath this piece, with both pieces right side up and so that the bottom edge of the new F16th sits as close as possible to the top of the first piece to avoid waste. Cut a line that follows the edge of the white bias strip, taking a small strip of fabric off the bottom of the new F16th (Fig 4).

8 Place the wavy edge of the new F16th right sides together with the white bias strip and sew together. You will need to constantly adjust both pieces of fabric so that their edges line up as you sew. Press open, pressing seams away from the white bias strip (Fig 5).

9 Trim a wavy line along this new piece approximately 1in x 2in wide, although it may be wider in places and narrower in others (Fig 6).

10 Sew a white bias 1in x 12in strip to this new wavy edge (Fig 7).

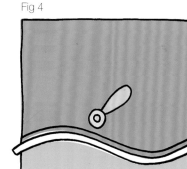

Fig 4

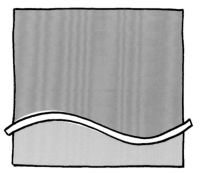

Fig 5

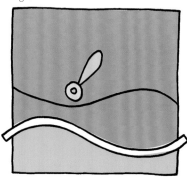

Fig 6

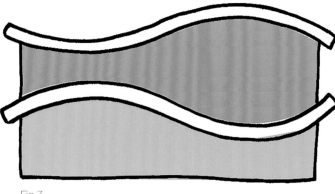

Fig 7

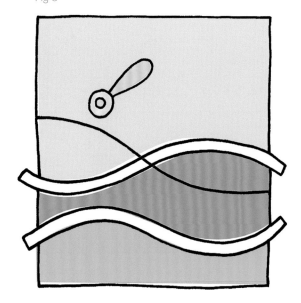

Fig 8

11 Continue adding white bias strips then new pieces of F16th sea fabric, until you have used nine sea F16ths and eight white bias strips between them. Sometimes when making the cut, your wavy cut may cross the white bias strip added just before (Fig 8). Note: When I made the sea blocks, I made the cuts more wavy, to suggest a turbulent sea. When I made the sky blocks, I made the cuts less wavy, to suggest a calm sky. Repeat to make all sixteen blocks.

12 Trim each block to 10in square. Spray starch may help to get the blocks to lie as flat as possible.

ASSEMBLING THE QUILT

13 Arrange the blocks into four rows of four, placing the twelve white 1in x 10in strips in between them. Sew each row together, pressing seams away from the blocks.

14 Now sew the four rows together using the three white 1in x 40in strips in between them. Press seams away from the blocks.

15 Sew the 2in x 40in border strips to the sides of the quilt. Press seams away from the blocks. Sew the 2in x 43in border strips to the top and bottom of the quilt. Press seams away from the blocks.

QUILTING AND FINISHING

16 Sew the two pieces of backing fabric together along the long sides using a ½in seam and press the seam open. Make a quilt sandwich of the quilt back (right side down), the batting and the quilt top (right side up) (see Techniques: Making a Quilt Sandwich, page 18).

17 Quilt as desired. The quilt shown is quilted with lots of wavy horizontal lines vaguely following the wavy lines on the piecing.

18 When all quilting is finished, square up the quilt, trimming the batting and backing (see Techniques: Squaring Up, page 19).

19 Sew the binding strips together end to end using diagonal seams or straight seams, as preferred. Press wrong sides together all along the length to make a double-fold binding. Bind the quilt to finish, taking care to miter the corners neatly (see Techniques: Making Binding Strips and Binding, pages 19 and 20).

Little Schoolhouses Wall Hanging

The schoolhouse quilt block is a classic, traditional block that works well in any fabrics. This charming wall hanging has six of these blocks in a simple arrangement with sashing and cornerstones, and the design is brought up to date with bright, modern print fabrics against a pale background.

Finished size
30in x 44in (76cm x 112cm) approx.

Notes
WOF = width of fabric
FPP = Foundation paper piecing
BKG = background
Use ¼in seams, unless instructed otherwise

Fabrics used
Quilt top: various scraps, plus Cream Linea by Makower UK
Quilt back and binding: Franklin by Denyse Schmidt for
   Freespirit Fabrics

You will need
- Fabrics for schoolhouses: scraps equivalent to eighteen 10in (25cm) squares
- Fabric for cornerstones: scraps equivalent to one 10in (25cm) square
- Background fabric: 1¼yds (1.25m)
- Backing fabric: 1⅛yds (1m)
- Batting: 38in x 52in (96cm x 132cm)
- Binding fabric: ⅜yd (0.3m)
- Six copies of the roof template (see pages 118–119)
- Coordinating piecing and quilting threads

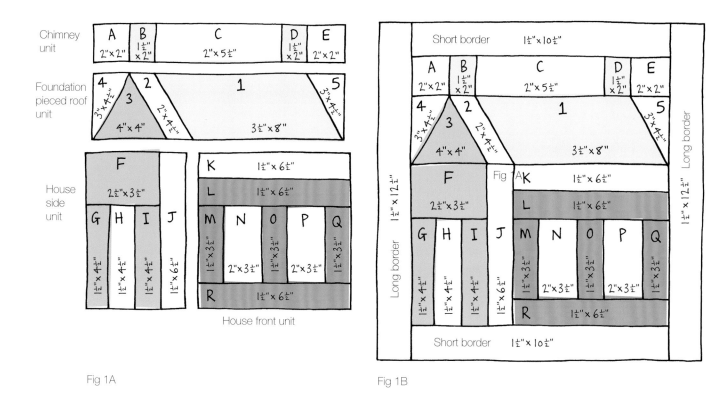

Fig 1A

Fig 1B

CUTTING

1 Organize the schoolhouse 10in squares or scraps into six groups of three similar colors—dark, medium and light. The four units of a block and the individual pieces are shown in Fig 1A, with each piece identified with a capital letter or number for foundation paper piecing. Fig 1B shows the whole block.

2 From each dark fabric, cut the following:
• Two 1½in x 6½in rectangles (pieces L and R).
• Three 1½in x 3½in rectangles (pieces M, O and Q).

3 From each medium fabric, cut the following:
• One 2½in x 3½in rectangle (piece F).
• Two 1½in x 4½in rectangles (pieces G and I).
• One 4in square (to foundation paper piece section 3 of the template).

4 From each light fabric, cut the following:
• Two 1½in x 2in rectangles (pieces B and D).
• One 3½in x 8in rectangle (to foundation paper piece section 1 of the template).

5 Cut twelve 2½in squares from the schoolhouse fabrics for the quilt cornerstones.

6 From the BKG fabric, cut ten 1½in x WOF strips and sub-cut as follows:
• Twelve 1½in x 6½in rectangles (pieces J and K).
• Six 1½in x 4½in rectangles (piece H).
• Twelve 1½in x 10½in rectangles (short border).
• Twelve 1½in x 12½in rectangles (long border).

7 From the BKG fabric, cut four 2in x WOF strips and sub-cut as follows:
• Six 2in x 5½in rectangles (piece C).
• Twelve 2in x 3½in rectangles (pieces N and P).
• Twelve 2in squares (pieces A and E).
• Six 2in x 4½in rectangles (to foundation paper piece section 2 of the template).

8 From the BKG fabric, cut six 2½in x WOF strips. Sub-cut into seventeen 2½in x 12½in rectangles for the sashing.

9 From the BKG fabric, cut two 3in x WOF strips. Sub-cut these strips into twelve 3in x 4½in rectangles (to foundation paper piece sections 4 and 5 of the template).

10 Cut the binding fabric into four 2½in x WOF strips.

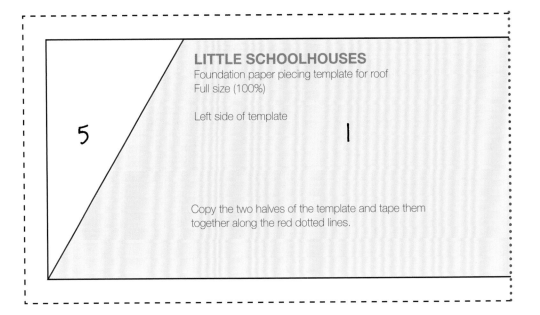

LITTLE SCHOOLHOUSES
Foundation paper piecing template for roof
Full size (100%)

Left side of template

5

I

Copy the two halves of the template and tape them
together along the red dotted lines.

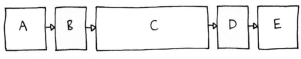

Fig 2 (Chimney unit)

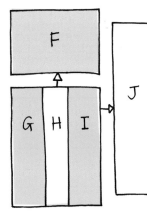

Fig 3 (House side unit)   Fig 4 (House front unit)

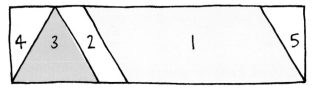

Fig 5 (Roof unit)

MAKING A SCHOOLHOUSE BLOCK

11 The making of the four block units is broken down into
steps—see Figs 1A and 1B on page 117.

12 Chimney unit: Sew pieces A, B, C, D and E together
(Fig 2).

13 House side unit: Sew G, H and I together (Fig 3). Sew F
to the top of this unit and then J to the right-hand side.

14 House front unit: Sew M, N, O, P and Q together (Fig 4).
Sew L and then K to the top of the unit and R to the bottom.

15 Roof unit: Foundation paper piece the template using one
BKG 2in x 4½in rectangle, two 3in x 4½in BKG rectangles,
the medium 4in square and the light 3½in x 8in rectangle
to make the unit shown in Fig 5. Refer to Techniques:
Foundation Paper Piecing, page 16, for full instructions and
diagrams on this technique.

ASSEMBLING THE BLOCK

16 Sew the chimney unit and roof unit together. Sew the
house side unit and house front unit together. Now sew the
bottom and the top of the house together (refer back to Fig 1B).

17 Sew the two short border strips to the top and bottom of
the block and press seams open or outwards. Sew the two
long border strips to the sides of the block and press seams
open or outwards (Fig 1B). The block should measure 12½in
square.

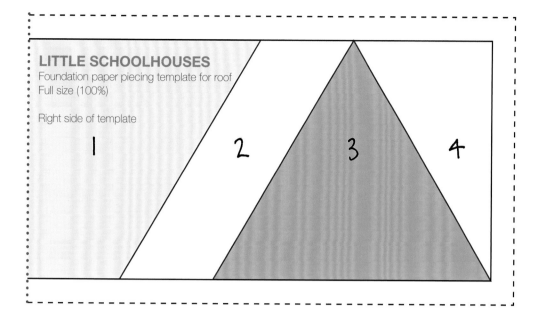

LITTLE SCHOOLHOUSES
Foundation paper piecing template for roof
Full size (100%)

Right side of template

1   2   3   4

---

18 Repeat steps 11 through 17 to make another five schoolhouse blocks.

ASSEMBLING THE QUILT

19 Sew the schoolhouse blocks, the 2½in square cornerstones and the 12½in sashing strips into rows as follows (Fig 6), pressing seams away from the sashing strips:
• Sew four rows, alternating cornerstones and sashing strips.
• Sew three rows, alternating sashing strips and schoolhouse blocks.

20 Sew the rows together, matching seams neatly. Press seams open or to one side.

QUILTING AND FINISHING

21 Make a quilt sandwich of the quilt back (right side down), the batting and the quilt top (right side up) (see Techniques: Making a Quilt Sandwich, page 18).

22 Quilt as desired. The quilt shown has a crosshatch pattern of wavy lines about 1¼in apart, using pale thread.

23 When all quilting is finished, square up the quilt, trimming the batting and backing (see Techniques: Squaring Up, page 19).

24 Sew the binding strips together end to end using diagonal seams or straight seams, as preferred. Press wrong sides together all along the length to make a double-fold binding.

Bind the quilt to finish, taking care to miter the corners neatly (see Techniques: Making Binding Strips and Binding, pages 19 and 20).

Fig 6

Cowboy Lap Blanket

The cowboy-themed fabrics in this quilt gave it the name, but any large-scale prints would work well in this pattern. Drunkard's Path blocks, classic blocks where a quarter circle sits inside a square, can be a bit tricky to piece, but these are so big that even quilters who haven't pieced curved seams before will find them quite manageable. This quilt comes together very quickly as there are only four blocks!

Finished size
38in (97cm) square approx.

Notes
WOF = width of fabric
Use ¼in seams, unless instructed otherwise

Fabrics used
Quilt top: Belmont by Erin Michael for Moda Fabrics
Quilt back and binding: Cream Linea by Makower UK

You will need
- Thirty-two 10in squares (a pre-cut pack such as a Moda Layer Cake is ideal)
- Backing fabric: 1¼yds (1.2m)
- Batting: 46in (117cm) square
- Binding fabric: ³⁄₈yd (0.3m)
- One each of templates A1, B1, A2 and B2 (see pages 124–125)
- Coordinating piecing and quilting threads

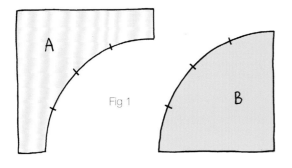

Fig 1

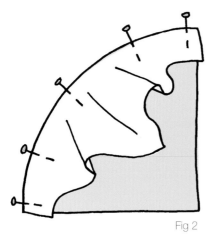

Fig 2

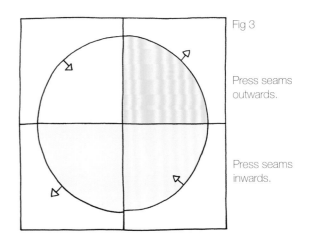

Fig 3

Press seams outwards.

Press seams inwards.

6 Sew along the seam, taking care to adjust the two pieces of fabric continuously so that the seam edges align all the way along the seam. Take your time, to avoid making any tucks in the seam. Do not press the seam at this point. This is one quarter block.

7 Once all sixteen quarter blocks are sewn together, you will need to decide on a layout before pressing the quarter block seams. Lay out all of the units to form circles and move them around until you are happy with the color arrangement. You can now press the curved seams, alternating whether the seams are pressed towards or away from template A, so when one quarter circle is pieced to the next quarter circle, the seams are pressed in opposite directions and will nest together nicely (Fig 3).

8 Sew the four rows of four blocks together, pressing seams in opposite directions. Now sew the four rows together to finish the quilt top.

CUTTING

1 First copy the four templates. Cut along the solid lines and then tape A1 and A2 together along those lines to make one A template. Repeat to make one B template.

2 Use these as a guide to cut sixteen A templates and sixteen B templates from the 10in squares.

3 Cut the binding fabric into four 2½in x WOF strips.

MAKING THE BLOCKS

4 Fold each cut piece in half and in half again and press the points where those folds meet the curved edge of each piece (see Fig 1). These creases mark midpoints and will help you sew the two curved pieces together.

5 Pin one A piece and one B piece (different fabrics) right sides together, with the A piece on top and making sure that the two pieces meet at each fold point and at the outer edges. Place the pins perpendicular to the seam edges (Fig 2). Use as many pins as needed to keep the curved edges together.

QUILTING AND FINISHING

9 Make a quilt sandwich of the quilt back (right side down), the batting and the quilt top (right side up) (see Techniques: Making a Quilt Sandwich, page 18).

10 Quilt as desired. The quilt shown was quilted with a crosshatch pattern of wavy lines about 2in apart, using pale thread.

11 When quilting is finished, square up the quilt, trimming the batting and backing (see Techniques: Squaring Up, page 19).

12 Sew the binding strips together end to end using diagonal seams or straight seams, as preferred. Press wrong sides together all along the length to make a double-fold binding. Bind the quilt to finish, taking care to miter the corners neatly (see Techniques: Making Binding Strips and Binding, pages 19 and 20).

Copy the template pieces and tape them
together along the solid red and dotted lines to
form Templates A and B.

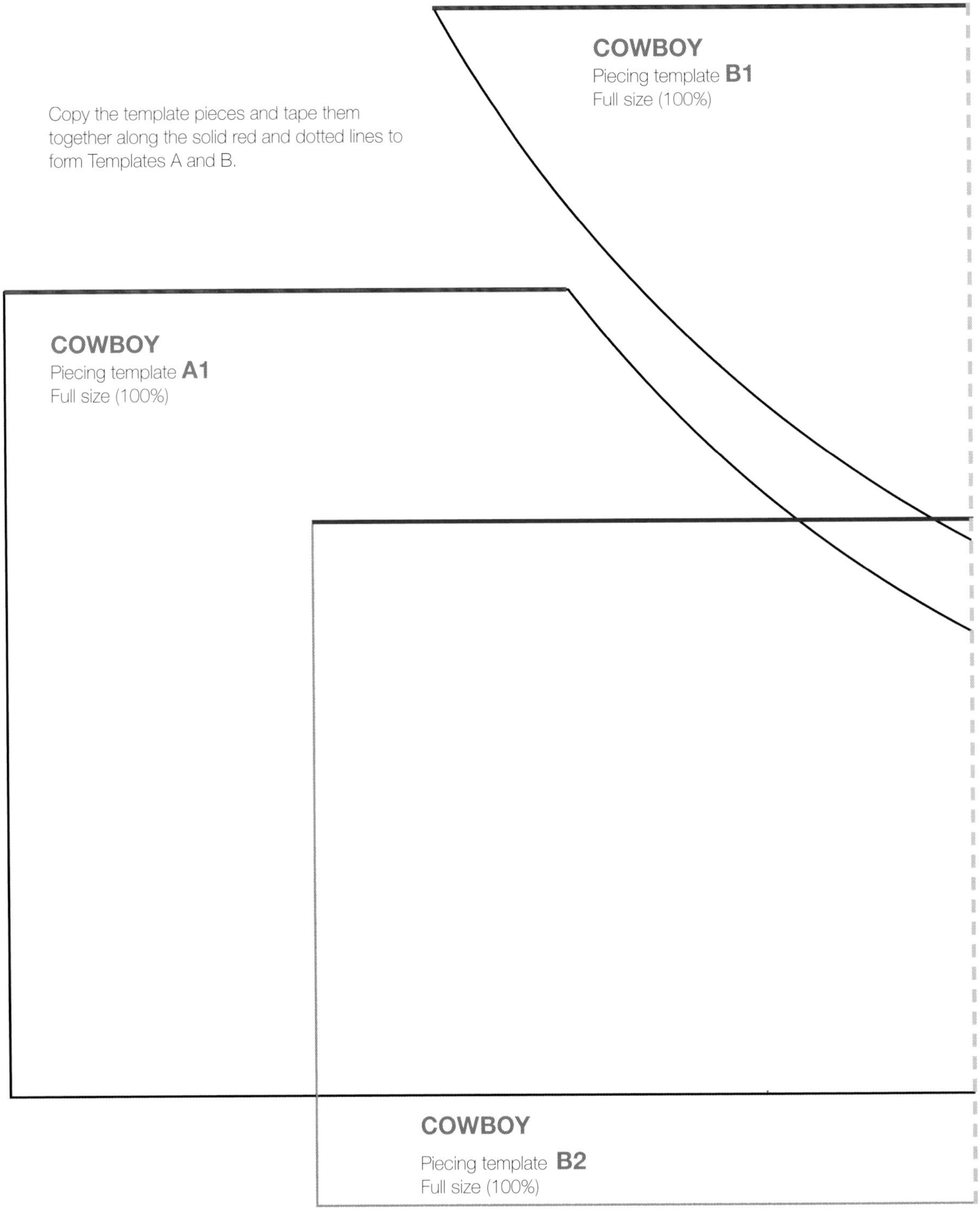

COWBOY
Piecing template **B1**
Full size (100%)

COWBOY
Piecing template **A1**
Full size (100%)

COWBOY
Piecing template **B2**
Full size (100%)

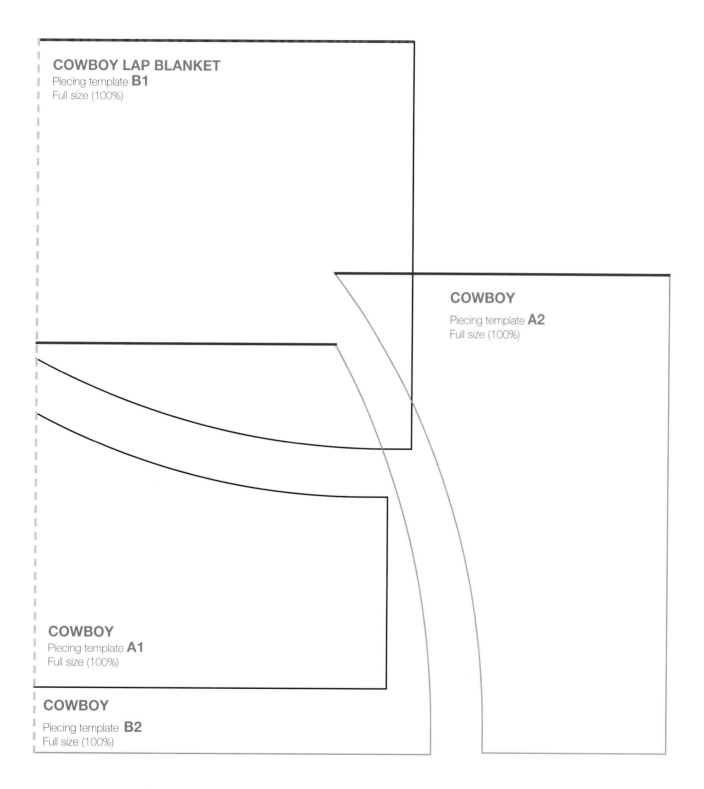

COWBOY LAP BLANKET
Piecing template **B1**
Full size (100%)

COWBOY
Piecing template **A2**
Full size (100%)

COWBOY
Piecing template **A1**
Full size (100%)

COWBOY
Piecing template **B2**
Full size (100%)

SUPPLIERS

Amitié Textiles, Australia
www.amitie.com.au

Ava & Neve (Liberty), Australia
www.avaandneve.com.au

Barn Yarns, UK
www.barnyarns.co.uk

Black Sheep Wools, UK
www.blacksheepwools.com

Bobbie Lou's Fabric Factory, US
www.bobbieloufabric.com

Celtic Fusions Fabrics, UK
www.celticfusionfabrics.com

Cotton Patch, UK
www.cottonpatch.co.uk

DuckaDilly, US
www.duckadilly.com

Eclectic Maker, UK
www.eclecticmaker.co.uk

Elephant In My Handbag, UK
www.elephantinmyhandbag.com

Fabric Please!, Canada
fabricplease.com

Fat Quarter Shop, US
www.fatquartershop.com

Fort Worth Fabric Studio, US
www.fortworthfabricstudio.com

Lady Belle Fabric, US
www.ladybellefabric.com

Lady Sew And Sew, UK
www.ladysewandsew.co.uk

Material Obsession, Australia
www.materialobsession.com.au

Peppermint Stitches, Australia
www.peppermintstitches.com.au

Pin It And Stitch, UK
www.pinitandstitch.co.uk

Pink Castle Fabrics, US
www.pinkcastlefabrics.com

Plush Addict, UK
www.plushaddict.co.uk

Purple Stitches, UK
www.purple-stitches.com

Quilter's Store, Australia
www.quiltersstore.com.au

Quiltessential, UK
www.quiltessential.co.uk

Quiltessentials, Australia
www.quiltessentials.com.au

Sew Hot, UK
www.sewhot.co.uk

Sew Me a Song, US
www.etsy.com/shop/sewmeasong

Shabby Fabrics, US
www.shabbyfabrics.com

Simply Solids, UK
simplysolids.co.uk

Voodoo Rabbit, Australia
www.voodoorabbit.com.au

Want it, Need it, Quilt it, Australia
www.wantitneeditquilt.com.au

Westwood Acres, US
www.westwoodacresfabric.com

MANUFACTURERS

Accuquilt die cutters
www.accuquilt.com

Art Gallery Fabrics
www.artgalleryfabrics.com

Aurifil Threads
www.aurifil.com

Cloud9 Fabrics
www.cloud9fabrics.com

Cotton + Steel Fabrics
www.cottonandsteelfabrics.com

Dashwood Studio
www.dashwoodstudio.com

Free Spirit Fabrics
www.freespiritfabrics.com

Makower Fabrics
www.makoweruk.com

Moda Fabrics
www.unitednotions.com

Oakshott Fabrics
www.oakshottfabrics.com

Riley Blake Designs
www.rileyblakedesigns.com

RJR Fabrics
www.rjrfabrics.com

Robert Kaufman Fabrics
www.robertkaufman.com

Rowan Fabrics
www.westminsterfabrics.com

Sizzix die cutters
www.sizzix.co.uk

Superior Titanium Topstitch Needles
www.superiorthreads.com

Windham Fabrics
www.windhamfabrics.net

ACKNOWLEDGMENTS

My work designing and making the projects and writing the patterns is only a fraction of the work that went into this book. First, I would like to thank my editor, Tara O'Sullivan, who has been the driving force and the vision behind the book, corralling my ideas and suggestions into a cohesive group of projects. She helped me to choose the photographer, the designer and the illustrator based on our conversations about how we would like the book to look and feel. And she has been endlessly patient and kind with my never-ending questions and concerns at every stage along the way. She and Kyle Books have made the whole process of writing this book, from start to finish, both rewarding and enjoyable.

I also want to pay tribute to the wonderful team that made the book look as good as it does—photographer Jan Baldwin, stylist Claudia Bryant, illustrator Bess Harding and designer Lucy Gowans. The photos have exactly the rich, eclectic look I had discussed with Tara, the illustrations are relaxed and fun, which was what I had always pictured for this book, and the design and layout are not only attractive but also clear and simple enough to be very usable.

My one special request when I started working on this book would be that Lin Clements would be the technical editor. I have worked with her on many projects in the past and love her incredible ability to pick out tiny details I've missed, to turn my instructions into something that's thorough and easy to understand and to be a lot of fun to work with along the way. Thank you, Lin, for making the toughest part of the whole book-writing process, the technical editing, a whole lot less stressful!

I would like to thank the suppliers and manufacturers who are listed at the back of the book, who have supported me by sponsoring my blog, lilysquilts.blogspot.com, or by providing me with the materials to make all the quilts in this book, and many more besides.

And last, but by no means least, I have to thank my husband and children because, without their endless support for what I do, I would not have been able to turn my hobby into my day job.